Best Lake Hikes Wisconsin

Best Lake Hikes
Wisconsin

A Guide to the State's Greatest Lake and River Hikes

Steve Johnson

GUILFORD, CONNECTICUT

FALCONGUIDES®

An imprint of The Rowman & Littlefield Publishing Group, Inc.
4501 Forbes Blvd., Ste. 200
Lanham, MD 20706
www.rowman.com

Falcon and FalconGuides are registered trademarks and Make Adventure Your Story is a trademark of The Rowman & Littlefield Publishing Group, Inc.

Distributed by NATIONAL BOOK NETWORK

Photos by Steve Johnson unless otherwise noted
Maps by The Rowman & Littlefield Publishing Group, Inc.

British Library Cataloguing in Publication Information available

Library of Congress Control Number: 2020950462

ISBN 978-1-4930-4680-5 (paper : alk. paper)
ISBN 978-1-4930-4681-2 (electronic)

∞™ The paper used in this publication meets the minimum requirements of American National Standard for Information Sciences—Permanence of Paper for Printed Library Materials, ANSI / NISO Z39.48-1992.

Contents

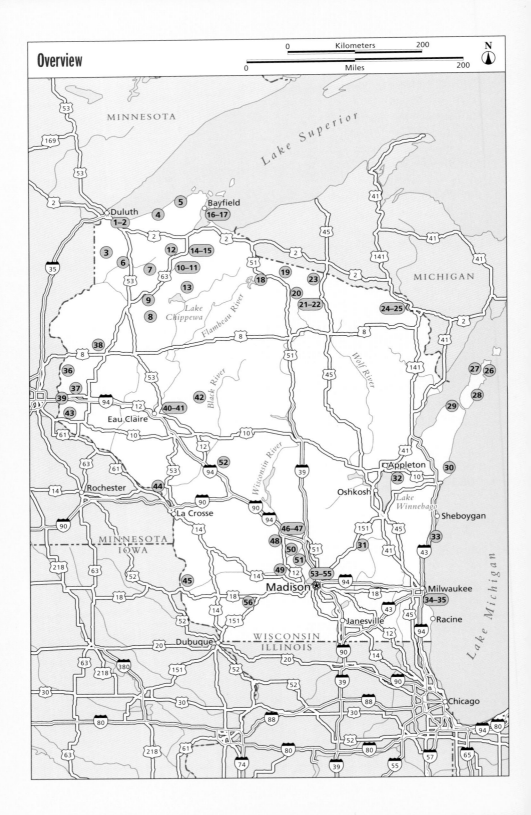

Overview

Acknowledgments

A book like this is a lot of fun to write. Traveling around the state hiking near wildly scenic lakeshore is not too bad a deal. But a book like this also requires the considerable talents of real pros. The aforementioned traveling and ogling is bookended by countless hours of research and editing.

I've been fortunate to work with the incomparable staff at Falcon for a bunch of years, and they nail it every time. Big thanks go to my editor David Legere for guiding this book from a good idea to a full-on celebration of Wisconsin's finest. One look at the maps on the following pages is all it takes to raise a glass to Melissa Baker. Her otherworldly skills turn my geographical scribbles into something you can actually use to find the hikes. All of Falcon's copy editors and the graphics gang are hereby granted enthusiastic applause from now until the end of time. You're all amazing.

Every time I write a where-to book like this, it is filled with priceless intel or anecdotes from an unexpected supporting cast. Thanks to the always-eager staff at our state and local parks, and the humble hiker on the Shattuck Trail who reminded me to veer left at the fork. The bartender at that little tavern with pale red paint and old-time Walter's sign hanging askew from a weathered log post knew a back way into that place out yonder. Fellow hikers all over the state who know a thing or two about finding real gems along the trails never hesitated to share their secrets.

Kent Merhar and Denice Breaux helped me stake out some of this book's best and captured them all to bring you frame-worthy photos throughout the book. Their work here is nothing short of inspirational, and the book is all the better for it. My heartfelt thanks to both of you.

My wingman and confidante and all-around badass Doug Earnest contributed incomparable photo-editing skills to select pages herein. You da man.

I would also like to pass along sincere gratitude to The Nature Conservancy, whose tireless commitment to conservation has preserved some of the world's most revered and critical lands. Several hikes in this book exist due to their influence.

Thank you, Mom and Dad, for keeping me fueled with rhubarb pie and fresh blueberries.

And special thanks to all of you for joining me in getting Out There.

Introduction

There's no denying we know how to make tasty cheese here in Wisconsin. Cows are held in high regard, and hardworking dairy farmers provide them with idyllic pastures on which to feast and enjoy lazy summer days. Less common knowledge, at least for nonlocals, is that our state is also a water lover's dream come true.

Two Great Lakes and more than 1,000 miles of their shorelines flank Wisconsin's northern and eastern sides. Within the state's borders, more than 15,000 lakes (sorry, Minnesota, we've got you beat) in a variety of sizes paint a good share of the state in shades of placid blue. Wisconsin also boasts nearly 13,000 rivers and streams, some small and quiet, others big and noisy. Even the state's name is derived from a river: French explorers Marquette and Joliet mentioned the Meskousing, a river name from the Native Miami language that passed through French and a transcription error to arrive at "Wisconsin." Who'd a thunk it?

Lots of this water is easily accessible from roadside parks, local picnic areas, or at the end of an easygoing hike. Some might require longer treks of a mile or three, and others are remote and mysterious, discovered only by backpacking your way through the great northern wilderness.

Whatever their shape, size, or location, all of our lakes and rivers have something special to offer. They each have a style and grace all their own—distinct personalities that inspire, enthuse, and seduce. Lake Superior, for example, might be restless and violent in the clutches of a November storm, while a secluded lake deep in the woods lies mirror flat and eerily quiet.

Whitefish Dunes State Park. Kent Merhar

Apostle Islands National Lakeshore.

Wisconsin's rivers are busy, darting around boulders and fallen logs, or they are elegant flows of velvety smooth swells. When visiting Wisconsin's lakes and rivers, look at how so many of them seem to match their surroundings. A lake in a big city seems to appear regal and cosmopolitan, complementing the tall buildings and go-get-'em lifestyle; a river in a forested, rocky gorge exudes a quieter, reflective beauty.

Join us on a tour of Wisconsin, from the dramatic bluffs and deep valleys of the Driftless Area to idyllic, undulating countryside in the state's midsection. Explore vibrant cities and quaint small towns. Lose yourself in the magic of Door County and breathe deeply of the incomparable northern forests. We'll explore lakes large and small and stroll with the currents of rivers, all the while uncovering lots of secrets and making acquaintance with some of the state's most dramatic liquid scenery.

This book is arranged by region from north to south and highlights the state's showiest lakes and rivers. A "best of" book is ultimately subjective, of course, implying that its contents include the finest examples of its title subject. I get to do it because my name's on the cover, and while your opinion might differ—"Why isn't our lake in the book?" or "What makes that little lake one of the best?"—I'm sharing with you places that genuinely inspired me and that I believe best represent our amazing state.

Each entry is introduced by an information block outlining the name and location of the water feature, hike distance and difficulty, applicable maps, GPS coordinates and directions to trailheads, contact information, and other beta. As far as gear and supplies, the best thing about these hikes is there are no complicated gear concerns. Just throw on decent footwear and proper clothing and away you go. Plan ahead, though, to make each visit a good one. Expect weather common to the area, and pack accordingly. Bring extra water in the humid heat of summer, and be ready for cold winds and impromptu rainstorms along the big lakes. On longer hikes your feet will be happier inside sturdy shoes or hiking boots, and take along snacks or a veritable grocery cart of grub for picnics at trailside overlooks or wooded campsites. Don't forget a camera or other photo device to take home the sights and sounds of lake country.

And stay safe around the water. Sometimes it's just plain irresistible to take one more step for a closer look, but that urge, especially near rivers and gorges, might send you on a long fall to a really hard or really wet landing.

As a Northland-bred scribe and tireless outdoor recreation junkie, it is a pleasure to share my explorations and ruminations, whatever your Dairyland State destination may be. My words are complemented by vivid, inspiring images from uber-talented Twin Cities photographers Kent Merhar and Denice Breaux. We hope you enjoy our efforts to bring you up close to Wisconsin's liquid landscapes. Let's go make some memories!

Glacier Trail—Chequamegon National Forest.

How to Use This Guide

This guide contains just about everything you need to choose, plan for, and enjoy a lake or river hike in Wisconsin. Packed with specific area information, *Best Lake Hikes Wisconsin* features sixty-two mapped and cued hikes leading to some of the state's best liquid landscapes, grouped together geographically.

Each hike starts with a short **summary** of the hike's highlights. These quick overviews give you a taste of the hiking adventures and featured locations. You'll learn about trail terrain and what unforgettable sights each route has to offer. Following the overview are **hike specs**—quick, nitty-gritty details:

Lake or river: The water feature appearing in the chapter.

Photogenic factor: This is a 1 to 5 rating, with 5 being slack-jaw gorgeous.

Distance: The total distance of the recommended route; out and back, loops, and lollipop routes are included in this guide.

Hiking time: The average time it will take to cover the route. It is based on the total distance, elevation gain, and condition and difficulty of the trail. Your fitness level will also affect your time.

Difficulty: Each hike has been assigned a level of difficulty; easy, moderate, or difficult. The rating system was developed from several sources and personal experience. These levels are meant to be a guideline only and may prove easier or harder for different people depending on ability and physical fitness. For purposes of this book, an easy hike will generally cover 2 miles or less total trip distance, with minimal elevation gain and a paved or smooth-surfaced dirt trail. A moderate hike will cover 3 to 5 miles total trip distance in one day, with moderate elevation gain and potentially rough terrain. A difficult hike may cover 5 or more miles total trip distance in one day, have difficult elevation gains, and/or have rough and/or rocky terrain.

Trail surface: General information about what to expect underfoot.

Other trail users: Such as horseback riders, mountain bikers, inline skaters, etc.

Canine compatibility: Know the trail regulations before you take your dog hiking with you. Dogs are typically allowed when leashed for the hikes in this book.

Land status: City park, state park, national park or forest, etc.

Fees and permits: Denotes park entrance fees and permits, if any. Permits available and fees payable online or at park ranger stations.

Maps: This is a list of other maps to supplement the maps in this book. USGS maps are the best source for accurate topographical information, but local park maps may show trails that are more recent. Use both.

Trail contacts: This is the location, phone number, and website for the local land manager(s) in charge of all the trails within the selected hike. Get trail access information before you head out, or contact the land manager after your visit if you see problems with trail erosion, damage, or misuse.

The **Finding the trailhead** section gives you dependable driving directions to trailheads. This also includes GPS trailhead coordinates for accurate navigation.

Rainbow Lake Wilderness.

The Hike is the meat of the chapter. Detailed and honest, it is a carefully researched impression of the lake or river, the hike, and interesting things you may see along the way, both natural and human. Under **Miles and Directions,** mileage cues identify all turns and trail-name changes, as well as points of interest. **Sidebars** are found throughout the book and are quick and often fascinating facts about the locale. A detailed and expertly crafted **map** is included with each hike and is derived from GPS tracks and related field data while on the hikes.

Enjoy your outdoor exploration of Wisconsin's beautiful lakes and rivers, and remember to pack out what you pack in.

How to Use the Maps

Overview map: This map shows the location of each hike in the area by hike number.

Route map: This is your primary guide to each hike. It shows the water featured, access roads and trails, points of interest, drinking water availability, landmarks, and geographical features. It also distinguishes trails from roads, and paved roads from unpaved roads. The selected route is highlighted, and directional arrows point the way.

Trail Finder

To get our readers started on the hikes best suited to their interests and abilities, this trail finder categorizes each of the hikes into a helpful list organized by hike number and name. Your favorite lakes or rivers might appear in more than one category.

Hike #/name	Large/popular lakes or rivers	Secluded locales	Easy-to-reach hikes	Kid-friendly hikes	Best hikes for backpackers
1 Wisconsin Point	■		■	■	
2 Osaugie Trail	■		■	■	
3 Pattison State Park		■	■		
4 Bear Beach State Natural Area	■		■		
5 Apostle Islands National Lakeshore	■				■
6 Brule Portage Trail	■		■	■	■
7 Tomahawk Lake Trails	■	■	■	■	
8 Green Lake Trail		■			
9 Hayward Recreational Forest		■	■	■	■
10 Glacier Trail—Chequamegon-Nicolet National Forest		■	■		■
11 Wilson Lake Trail—Chequamegon-Nicolet National Forest		■	■	■	■
12 Rainbow Lake Wilderness—North Country Trail		■			■

Trail	1	2	3	4	5
13 Porcupine Lake Wilderness—North Country Trail	■			■	
14 Copper Falls State Park—Doughboys Trail	■	■	■	■	■
15 Penokee Range—North Country Trail	■		■		
16 Madeline Island—Big Bay State Park	■	■	■	■	■
17 Madeline Island Wilderness Preserve	■		■		■
18 North Lakeland Discovery Trails		■	■		■
19 Van Vliet Hemlocks State Natural Area		■	■	■	
20 Fallison Lake Trail		■	■	■	
21 Star Lake Trail and Plum Lake Hemlock Forest SNA					■
22 Franklin Lake Trail		■	■		■
23 Catherine Wolter Wilderness Trails			■	■	
24 Lauterman Lake Trail	■		■	■	
25 Perch Lake Trail	■		■	■	
26 Newport State Park		■	■		■
27 Peninsula State Park—Nicolet Loop		■	■		■
28 Whitefish Dunes State Park		■	■		■

Hike #/name	Large/popular lakes or rivers	Secluded locales	Easy-to-reach hikes	Kid-friendly hikes	Best hikes for backpackers
29 Potawatomi State Park	■		■	■	
30 Point Beach State Forest	■		■	■	
31 Horicon National Wildlife Refuge		■	■	■	
32 High Cliff State Park	■		■	■	
33 Kohler-Andrae State Park	■		■	■	
34 Seven Bridges Trail	■	■	■	■	
35 Milwaukee Lakefront Trail	■		■	■	
36 Interstate State Park	■		■	■	
37 Willow River State Park	■		■	■	
38 Straight Lake State Park—Ice Age Trail		■	■		■
39 Lakefront Park	■		■	■	
40 Chippewa Moraine State Recreation Area—Ice Age Trail		■	■	■	■
41 Brunet Island State Park		■	■	■	
42 Mondeaux Esker—Aldo Leopold and Ice Age Trails	■	■	■	■	■
43 Kinnickinnic State Park	■		■	■	

Site	Column 1	Column 2	Column 3	Column 4
44 Perrot State Park		■		■
45 Wyalusing State Park		■		■
46 Chapel Gorge Trail—Dells of the Wisconsin River SNA	■	■	■	■
47 Wisconsin Dells Scenic Riverwalk	■	■		■
48 Echo-Lakeview Loop—Mirror Lake State Park		■		
49 Ferry Bluff SNA—Cactus Bluff Trail		■	■	
50 Devil's Lake State Park		■		■
51 Gibraltar Rock State Natural Area—Ice Age Trail		■	■	
52 Black River State Forest		■	■	
53 Lakeshore Nature Preserve—UW Madison	■	■		■
54 University of Wisconsin Arboretum	■	■		■
55 Pheasant Branch Conservancy	■	■	■	
56 Governor Dodge State Park		■	■	■

Map Legend

Transportation

≡≡(43)≡≡	Interstate Highway
≡(53)≡	US Highway
≡(35)≡	State Road
≡(91)≡	Local/County Road
=== :	Gravel Road
⊢———⊣	Railroad
— ·· — ·	State Boundary

Trails

-------	Featured Trail
————	Paved Trail
------	Trail or Fire Road

Water Features

⬭	Body of Water
⌇	River/Creek
⌐	Spring
⋛	Waterfall

Land Management

▣	National Park/Forest
▣	National Monument/ Wilderness Area
▭	State/County Park

Symbols

✕	Airport
⌣	Bridge
■	Building/Point of Interest
≋	Boat Ramp
⫴⫴⫴	Boardwalk
⋀	Campground
▲	Campsite (backcountry)
⊟	Inn/Lodging
ⵢ	Lighthouse
℗	Parking
⊞	Picnic Area
⬚	Ranger Station/Park Office
⑪	Restaurant
⬕	Scenic View
○	Town
㉑	Trailhead
�𝕀	Tower
⊢——⊣	Tunnel
❷	Visitor/Information Center

Far North and Lake Superior Shore

Even a single visit leaves its mark. Seeing the big lake up close is an experience, an indelible memory that remains with you like your own shadow. You will return to the water, for the lake's powerful siren song echoes in your soul, and to hear it best is to be at its side.

Poetic musing aside, for anyone hailing from the Northland, Lake Superior is part of our lives. The lake captivates us from childhood and its spell melds with our souls. Visitors are fascinated and struck by its beauty and leave here inspired and humbled. Superior is stunningly beautiful. It is moody and seductive. It is a maelstrom, peace, challenge, inspiration. It is the *Fitz* and Gordon Lightfoot. Deep and icy cold.

Driftwood detritus on the shore, Wisconsin Point.

Pattison State Park. DENICE BREAUX

As we are traditionally, instinctively, excitedly inclined to do around here, we get out to these places to feel and touch and smell and just be, and Lake Superior invites us to its waters and shores to breathe deep of wild. The big lake grabs hold of its audiences, be it an innocent child tossing polished round rocks from a beach or the hardened crew of an immense freighter battling 30-foot swells. Even in its absence, the mighty lake's hypnotic waters remain saturated in our memories.

Lake Superior's southern shoreline is a conduit to our daydreams: a long and winding journey from the Twin Ports to Bayfield and the Apostle Islands; through magical lands of quiet bays; high, rugged cliffs, and scenic rivers. In springtime, boisterous rivers blast over crests of high cliffs into unforgettable vistas. Autumn sees tranquil creeks whisper beneath rustic bridges and past secret hideaways.

In winter the big lake heaves and growls as its deathly cold waters recklessly pile 3-foot-thick hunks of ice in haphazard piles along the shore. October and November bring storms and Superior builds into a howling fury, tossing around thousand-foot ships like bathtub toys and slamming roiling, frothy waves into anything in their way before reluctantly surrendering to battered but stalwart shoreline. It is an incredible, life-list experience to be near the lake when it turns wild and surly.

Lake Superior's southern shore boasts more than 300 miles of drop-dead gorgeous scenic sights, quaint towns, and verdant forests. It is decorated with hundreds of dazzling inland lakes and rivers as well, offering some of the very best in liquid North Country scenery.

1 Wisconsin Point

Hunt for driftwood, sink your toes in the sand, and rub shoulders with the grand-daddy of the Great Lakes on this easygoing beach hike.

Lake or river: Lake Superior
Photogenic factor: 5+
Distance: The point is 3.0 miles end to end. This hike is about strolling the beach with panoramic lake views. Choose whatever distance suits you.
Difficulty: Easy
Hiking time: 30 minutes to all day
Trail surface: Sandy beach, with scattered driftwood and small rocks

Other trail users: Hikers only
Canine compatibility: Leashed pets allowed
Land status: City of Superior
Fees and permits: None
Maps: Various city maps; USGS Superior
Trail contacts: Superior Chamber and Visitors Bureau, 205 Belknap St., Superior 54880; (715) 394-7716; superiorchamber.org

Finding the trailhead: At Superior's eastern fringe at US 53 and Moccasin Mike Road, follow Moccasin Mike Road 1.4 miles east to Wisconsin Point Road. Turn left on Wisconsin Point Road and head 2 miles to the first turnout parking area. Access the beach here or from any other parking area along the road. **Trailhead GPS:** N46 68.654' / W91 97.367'

The Hike

On a warm summer day with a light breeze kicking up its heels, strolling the shore of Lake Superior is a soothing elixir for the soul. Visiting during the icy grip of an irritable, howling November nor'easter hurling about foamy, death-cold waves is humbling and frightening. Wisconsin Point is your front-row seat for every performance.

The Ojibwa called her *gitchi-gami*, the great sea. They were right, as this is indeed a very special place and one of my favorite destinations in the state to hike. It's more about wandering free, with every one of my senses in overdrive. Front and center, of course, is the immense beauty of Lake Superior, the largest freshwater lake in the world.

Let's talk a minute about just how big it is. The lake's surface area is about the size of South Carolina, and its deepest point plunges to more than 1,300 feet. There's enough water out there to cover all of North and South America to a foot deep! It's damned cold too. Although climate change is messing up the works, Superior's water temperature well below the surface still hovers around 39°F. *Brrrr.*

For awestruck kids hailing from these parts, Lake Superior is our first chance to see what an ocean looks like. I was one of those kids, and even all grown up, I'm still spellbound by this place. It is equal parts enchanting and frightening, inviting and foreboding. I've seen the lake as tranquil and flat as an endless Kansas highway, and raging in bone-chilling, roaring fury. Both versions are life-list moments.

Hiking along muddy spring waters.

Just like the little kid version of me, I can still look out over the big lake in rapt wonder and do so every chance I get. Wisconsin Point is a go-to destination for everything great about Lake Superior. From one of the parking areas along the road, trails over humps of sand dunes or through the stretch of pine woods allow easy access to the beach. From there, it's all up to you. Wander the sandy beach and dodge incoming waves, stretch out in the tallgrasses and watch clouds chug by, or sit on a hunk of grizzled driftwood and lose yourself to the horizon. The views are spectacular in all directions. The ore docks of Superior and Duluth are right over there, with Canal Park and the lift bridge way in the distance, Duluth's rugged hills, and a long stretch of the majestic North Shore.

And there's a lighthouse as a bonus. Head down to the end of Wisconsin Point Road and walk the breakwater out to the Superior Entry lighthouse. You can't go inside, but the view from out there is outta sight. In winter and spring it's fun to walk

Wisconsin Point

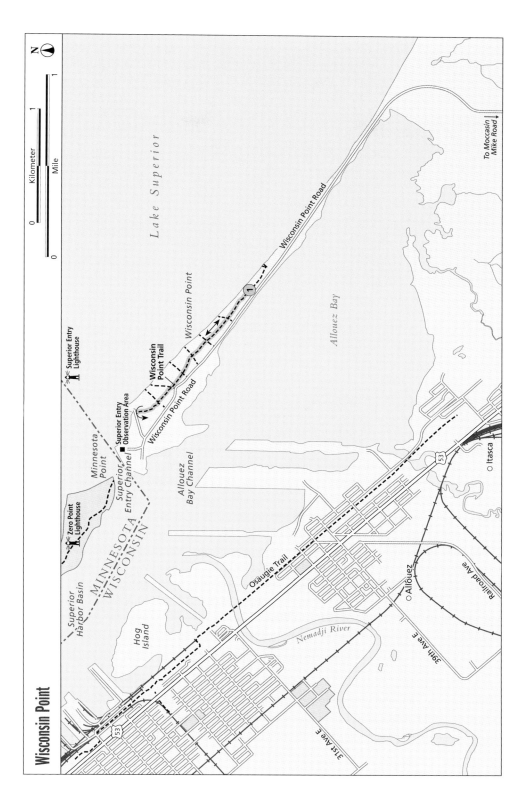

N

Kilometer
0   1   1

0   1
Mile

Lake Superior

Wisconsin Point Road

Wisconsin Point

Wisconsin Point

Wisconsin
Point Trail

1

Allouez Bay

Superior Entry
Lighthouse

*Minnesota
Point*

Superior Entry
Observation Area

Wisconsin Point Road

*Allouez
Bay Channel*

Zero Point
Lighthouse

Superior
Entry Channel

MINNESOTA
WISCONSIN

Superior Harbor Basin

*Hog
Island*

Osaugie Trail

Nemadji River

53

Itasca

Allouez

Railroad Ave

39th Ave E

31st Ave E

53

To Moccasin
Mike Road

Wisconsin Point Lighthouse and distant Duluth skyline.

along the entry pier and watch massive wedges of ice heave and crack and growl like some kind of colossal, watery beast. Speaking of winter, be sure to visit in the coldest months (there are a lot of them) to experience the point in a new and frosty light, when the lake sloughs off massive shards of ice 2 feet thick and heaps them in haphazard piles along the shore.

Miles and Directions

0.0 Wisconsin Point stretches roughly 3 miles end to end. Do the whole thing or start at any of the access points and wander as long as you like. Chase incoming waves, explore rolling sand dunes, or hike the path through the pine woods flanking the beach.

0.8 Arrive at the lighthouse breakwater.

1.6 Trailhead area of the beach. Continue hiking to the natural end of the beach and turn around.

3.0 Arrive back at the trailhead.

LIGHTING THE WAY

In the late 1800s the natural opening between Wisconsin and Minnesota Points served as entry for all shipping traffic into the Twin Ports. The Superior Entry Lighthouse was commissioned in June of 1913, safely guiding more than 900 vessels in and out of Superior Bay. The light's location is situated on a 10-mile-long sandbar (the longest freshwater bar in the world) that runs between the Duluth and Superior ports, making this one of the world's safest shipping harbors. Wisconsin Point is also on the National Register of Historic Places and the lighthouse is now privately owned.

2 Osaugie Trail

This easygoing hike is steeped in cover-shot views every step of the way and passes by two historical museums.

Lake or river: Superior Bay	**Canine compatibility:** Leashed pets allowed
Photogenic factor: 5	**Land status:** City of Superior
Distance: 2.0 miles out and back to the Bong	**Fees and permits:** None
Historical Center	**Maps:** Various city maps; USGS Superior
Difficulty: Easy	**Trail contacts:** Superior Chamber and Visitors
Hiking time: 45-60 minutes	Bureau, 205 Belknap St., Superior 54880;
Trail surface: Paved pathway	(715) 394-7716; superiorchamber.org
Other trail users: Cyclists, inline skaters	

Finding the trailhead: The hike starts at the trailside park at 18th Avenue and East 2nd Street (US 2/53). **Trailhead GPS:** N46 71.169' / W92 05.335'

The Hike

While Wisconsin Point is wild nature, the Osaugie Trail is calm and civilized, but the outrageous views are no less impressive here in town. A teaser look at Superior Bay greets hikers right from the trailhead, and it gets better with every step. About 100 yards from the start, the marina at Barker's Island comes into view, where water in the bay reflects from a contingent of silver masts held strong by dozens of skiffs.

Barker's is a man-made island, created by Captain Charles S. Barker with sand and other assorted debris from canal-dredging operations in the late 1800s. The location of the island is another story altogether. One legend has it that it was simply too expensive to haul all that dredge sand out of the harbor by tug. Another tale holds more devious undertones, born of the feud between Barker and lumber baron Martin Pattison. The story goes that Barker dumped everything in that exact spot to spoil the view from Pattison's waterfront mansion. Whatever the case, Barker's Island today is one of Superior's go-to tourist destinations.

The Osaugie Trail makes barely-there undulations on its westward track to the entrance to the island, which conveniently provides easy access to another staple of Superior history, the SS *Meteor* Maritime Museum. A fixture in Superior since 1973, the museum provides a look at a fascinating chapter of Great Lakes shipping.

Continue on a final, gentle curve to the turnaround point at the Richard Bong Veterans Historical Center. Plan some time to check out this local gem, packed with engaging exhibits and military relics. Bong was born in Superior and grew up in the little town of Poplar, 20 miles east of here. He joined the Army Air Corps in 1941 and just three years later already held the reputation as an ace. Bong went on to record

Sailing on Superior Bay.

Easygoing lakeside stroll.

twenty-seven victories in the air and received the Congressional Medal of Honor in 1944. He died a year later when his plane exploded on a test flight, the same day the Enola Gay dropped the atomic bomb over Hiroshima.

On the return trip take a moment to reflect on the history of the trail itself. Joseph Osaugie was a leader of the Fond du Lac band of Ojibwa and chief of an Ojibwa

Osaugie Trail

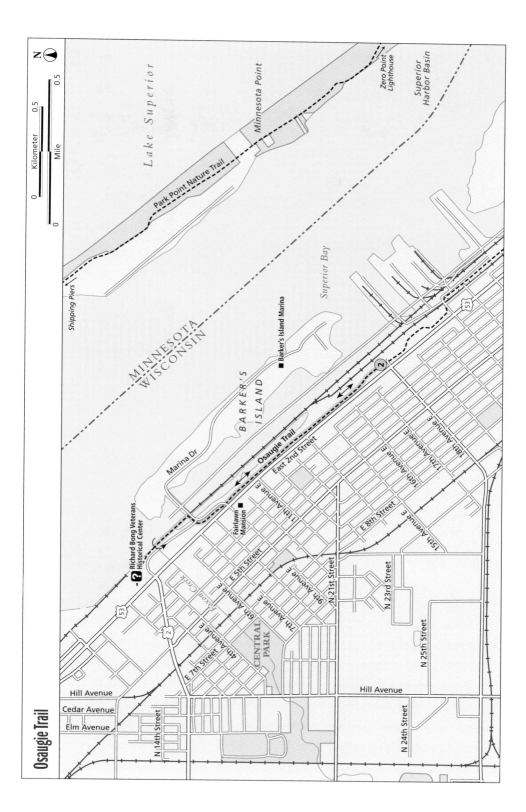

N

Kilometer
0   0.5
Mile
0   0.5

Lake Superior

Shipping Piers

Park Point Nature Trail

Minnesota Point

Zero Point
Lighthouse

Superior
Harbor Basin

MINNESOTA
WISCONSIN

Superior Bay

BARKER'S
ISLAND

Barker's Island Marina

Marina Dr

Osaugie Trail

East 2nd Street

Richard Bong Veterans
Historical Center

Fairlawn Mansion

11th Avenue E

Nixon Creek

CENTRAL
PARK

E 5th Street

E 7th Street

4th Avenue E

5th Avenue E

6th Avenue E

7th Avenue E

9th Avenue E

N 21st Street

N 23rd Street

N 25th Street

E 8th Street

15th Avenue E

16th Avenue E

17th Avenue E

18th Avenue E

Hill Avenue

Hill Avenue

Cedar Avenue

Elm Avenue

N 14th Street

N 24th Street

53

2

2

Barker's Island Marina and Duluth skyline.

village that made its primary home on Wisconsin Point, in addition to several other locations around today's Douglas County.

Back at the trailhead, consider a future hike or bike ride along the rest of the 10-mile Osaugie Trail. Historical nugget: About 2 miles east, the trail passes beneath the immense span of the Burlington Ore Dock. This is where the legendary *Edmund Fitzgerald* took on its load of iron ore before heading out into a ferocious November gale that would ultimately be the gallant freighter's final voyage.

Miles and Directions

0.0   From the trailhead at US 2/53, hike the paved trail northwest.

0.1   Pass Barker's Island Marina off your right shoulder.

0.6   Pass entrance to the marina and SS *Meteor* Maritime Museum. The trail curves toward the bay and then the homestretch to the halfway point.

1.0   Arrive at the Bong Museum. Return to the trailhead the same way.

2.0   Arrive at the trailhead.

THE SS *METEOR*

The unconventional design of the whaleback steamers allowed the workhorse ships to carry a great amount of cargo with minimum draft. One of only forty-four whalebacks built in the late 1800s, the 336-foot *Meteor* was originally named *Frank Rockefeller* and later *South Park*. The ship served as a dredge and auto carrier and hauled gasoline and other liquids for a quarter century before running aground in Michigan in 1969. As the last remaining whaleback, *Meteor* escaped the scrapyard and became a museum in 1973. Today it is a National Historic Landmark and popular area attraction.

3 Pattison State Park

Score choice views of ruggedly elegant Big Manitou Falls and hike bridges and boardwalks on this scenic tour in one of Wisconsin's most popular state parks.

Lake or river: Black River and Interfalls Lake
Photogenic factor: 4
Distance: 2.0-mile loop for Beaver Trail (also known as Beaver Slide Trail); 0.1 mile to Big Manitou Falls
Difficulty: Easy
Hiking time: About 75 minutes for Beaver Trail loop
Trail surface: Paved and packed gravel and dirt

Other trail users: Hikers only
Canine compatibility: Leashed pets allowed
Land status: State park
Fees and permits: Vehicle pass required
Maps: State park map; USGS Sunnyside
Trail contacts: Pattison State Park, 6294 S. State Rd. 35, Superior 54880; (715) 399-3111; dnr.wi.gov/topic/parks/name/pattison/

Finding the trailhead: From Belknap Street in downtown Superior, follow Tower Avenue (WI 35) south for 13 miles to the park entrance. **Trailhead GPS:** N46 53.667' / W92 11.925'

The Hike

This hike packs a punch right from the start, with the roar and classic North Country beauty of 165-foot Big Manitou Falls, Wisconsin's highest falls and the tallest east of the Mississippi. A short spur trail from the parking area leads to several observation

Big Manitou Falls. DENICE BREAUX

Fall colors on the trail. DENICE BREAUX

points overlooking the falls. Keep your camera at the ready to capture postcard (remember those?) shots and then retrace your tracks to the parking and picnic area.

Look for the trailhead sign for the Beaver Slide, Little Manitou, and Logging Camp Trails at the top side of Interfalls Lake. A gentle slope with a collection of benches treats park visitors to balcony views of the placid lake and surrounding forest of pine, birch, aspen, and maple. Cross a short wooden bridge and follow the gravel and dirt path southbound. Keep an eye out for some of the 200 species of critters that call this area home, including bald eagles, moose, black bear, white-tailed deer, songbirds of dozens of shapes and sizes, pileated woodpeckers, and elusive timber wolves.

This area was also home to Native American tribes and the site of an 1800s-era trading post, mining operations, and a logging camp built by the park's namesake, Martin Pattison. In fact, it is thanks to Pattison that this splendid area and the falls themselves are here at all (see sidebar).

THE PARK THAT ALMOST WASN'T

In 1917 a plan to build a power dam on the Black River nearly succeeded, and the ensuing giant lake would have swallowed Big Manitou Falls, erasing it right off the map. Lumber and mining baron Martin Pattison didn't care for the idea and quietly purchased nearly 700 acres of land from private owners in the area to squash the proposed dam. A year later he donated the land to the state, allowing the creation of today's park named in his honor.

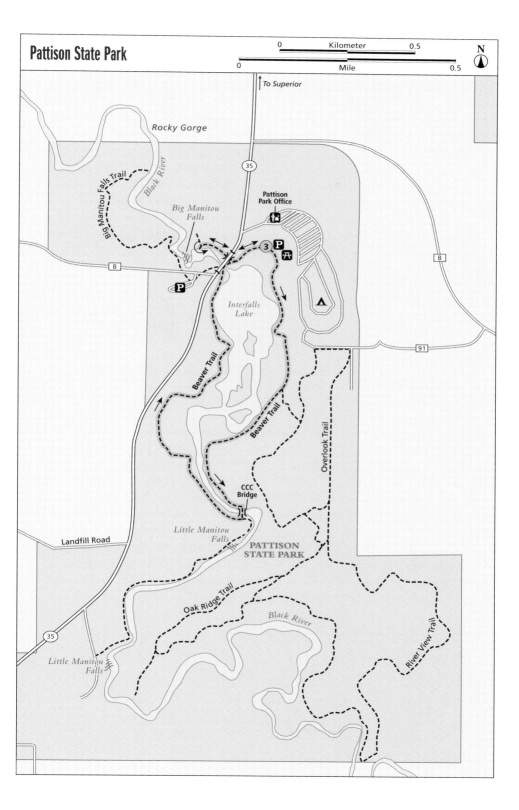

Pattison State Park

Kilometer
0   0.5

Mile
0   0.5

N

To Superior

Rocky Gorge

Black River

Big Manitou Falls Trail

35

Big Manitou Falls

Pattison Park Office

3

P

P

B

B

Interfalls Lake

Beaver Trail

Beaver Trail

Overlook Trail

91

CCC Bridge

Little Manitou Falls

PATTISON STATE PARK

Landfill Road

Oak Ridge Trail

Black River

River View Trail

35

Little Manitou Falls

Views of the lake appear through breaks in stands of noble, deep-green spruce as the trail meanders along the east shore. Look for the trio of small islands out there as the path makes a gentle C turn to the junction with a Civilian Conservation Corps bridge crossing the Black River.

The masterful stonework, masonry, and all-around outdoor artistry seen in this bridge and many other parks throughout Wisconsin and the nation are courtesy of the Civilian Conservation Corps (CCC). Born of President Franklin D. Roosevelt's work relief program in 1933, the CCC provided work for millions of Great Depression–era young men and instilled a nationwide awareness of natural resources conservation. Of the many significant accomplishments of this stalwart group, the CCC planted nearly *3 billion* trees in America's reforestation efforts. That's good stuff.

On the other side of the bridge, turn right and follow close to the river and marshy lowlands on a squiggly course to the pedestrian walkway over the dam and a final short stretch back to the trailhead.

Miles and Directions

0.0 From the picnic shelter, hike the paved path through the tunnel under the highway to observation points with great views of Big Manitou Falls. Return to the shelter to begin the main loop.

0.2 From the shelter, hike south past the bathhouse and swimming beach. Note that signage labels this trail as the Beaver Slide Trail.

0.9 Catch glimpses of clumps of wooded islands redirecting the Black River in various directions.

1.2 Cross the CCC bridge over the river and loop back north.

2.0 Cross the pedestrian walkway over the dam, which regulates river flow into Interfalls Lake.

2.2 Arrive back at the trailhead.

4 Bear Beach State Natural Area

Feed your wanderlust and get up-close lake views every step of the way on this secluded beach walk. **Note:** "Up-close" means right in the water at creek crossings. Use caution and be prepared to get wet.

Lake or river: Lake Superior
Photogenic factor: 5
Distance: 3.8 miles out and back
Difficulty: Easy to moderate
Hiking time: About 2 hours
Trail surface: Sand
Other trail users: None

Canine compatibility: Leashed pets allowed
Land status: State forest
Fees and permits: None
Maps: USGS Cloverland
Trail contacts: Brule River State Forest, 6250 Ranger Rd., Brule 54820; (715) 372-5678; dnr.wi.gov

Finding the trailhead: From US 2 in Maple, head north on CR F 4 miles to WI 13. Turn left and go 0.5 mile to Becks Road (gravel). Follow Becks Road 5 miles north. Parking is available in a small space on a bluff overlooking the lake, as well as 0.1 mile farther up the road toward the lake. **Trailhead GPS:** N46 89.952' / W92 43.699'

The Hike

Remote, no crowds, and wave-song. Can't beat that trifecta for an afternoon stroll along Lake Superior's shore. It all comes together on this hiking adventure at Bear Beach State Natural Area (SNA) at the top end of Brule River State Forest.

Wisconsin's SNA program was the first state-sponsored conservation effort of its kind and today includes nearly *700* natural areas, from tiny, 1-acre parcels to sites of several thousand acres. SNAs are vital links in the protection of endangered flora and fauna, geologic interests, and biodiversity of our state's indigenous lands. The Bear Beach SNA includes 5 miles of natural and undeveloped sand beach, with upland forest of birch, aspen, alder, and scattered pine. The estuaries of many creeks and tributaries attract the likes of terns, snow buntings, gulls, and other shorebirds, as well as black bears and wolves. It is a rare treat to experience this kind of untouched habitat along Lake Superior's shoreline.

But I'll start with a caveat: While this is a great place to really feel the big lake's sounds and legendary beauty and its many moods, it can also be a dangerous place. The beach here is narrow, commonly littered with deadfall and chaotic piles of driftwood, and rapidly disappears during storms or high water. Creek crossings along the way invoke a Lewis and Clark spirit, but wading across can turn from knee-deep to waist deep to full-on swimming. In fact, depending on the state of random barriers and state of the lake, it might not even be possible to complete the entire hike. Keep your common sense firing, watch the weather, and be prepared.

Lake Superior and Duluth in the far distance.

That said, in a state of repose or fury, Lake Superior has inspired me since I staggered near its shore as a toddler. Discovering Bear Beach many years later rekindled that unfettered spirit, and those of you of like mind will appreciate this quote that so elegantly describes the feeling:

> There is a pleasure in the pathless woods,
> there is a rapture on the lonely shore,
> there is a society where none intrudes,
> by the deep sea and music in its roar:
> I love not man the less, but nature more.

Cheers to Lord Byron for putting words to what many of us feel when near Lake Superior.

Filled with soulful inspiration, I like to start this lake hike with a short stroll to the west, just to see the latest collection of driftwood and check out the beauteous views of Duluth and Superior. And I always seem to linger like a statue along the way and look far north to the lake's North Shore. Captivating.

The hike begins in earnest right from the trailhead, with a ford of the mouth of Pearson Creek. This is typically an easy one, but again, always be ready for a challenge. Cruise along the shore for about one-half mile to creek crossing number two at Haukkala Creek, making its final passage from pastoral lands far inland. There's

Bear Beach State Natural Area

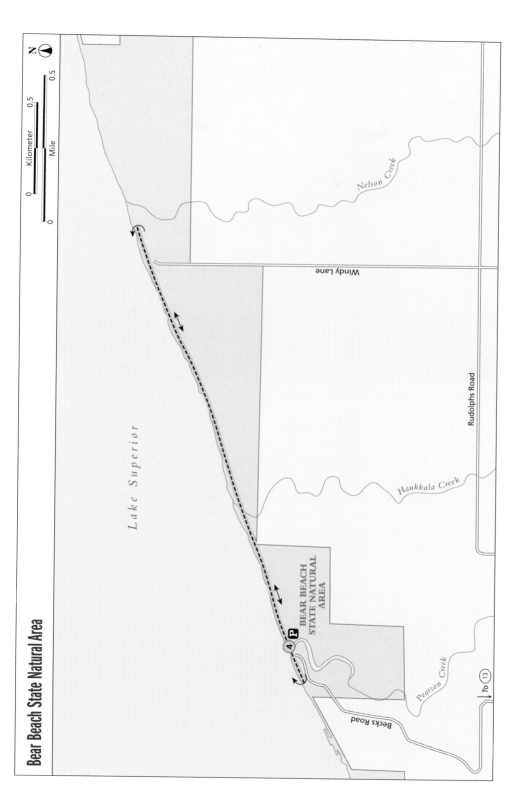

N

0 Kilometer 0.5

0 Mile 0.5

Lake Superior

Nelson Creek

Windy Lane

Rudolphs Road

Haukkala Creek

BEAR BEACH
STATE NATURAL
AREA

P

4

Pearson Creek

Becks Road

To 13

Driftwood chaos along the shore.

usually a huge melee of driftwood of all sizes hereabouts that may require climbing, scrambling, and shinnying. You can make this a turnaround point or keep on truckin'.

The next mile is generally easier hiking, save for a handful of little creeks and unexpected driftwood barriers. The next major obstacle is Nelson Creek and the turnaround point. It's entirely possible to continue on roughly another 5 miles to the mouth of the Bois Brule River, but it's not recommended without transportation planned and waiting. Nearly 18 round-trip miles of challenging beach walking with wet feet (or worse) is a bit much. Or is it?

From Nelson Creek, follow the beach back to the trailhead.

Miles and Directions

0.0 From the trailhead, wander the beach westward a bit for views of Duluth and Superior, and then head back to Pearson Creek.

0.2 Ford the mouth of Pearson Creek.

0.7 At the junction with Haukkala Creek, cross it and keep heading east.

1.9 At the junction with Nelson Creek, turn around here and retrace your tracks.

3.8 Arrive at the trailhead.

5 Apostle Islands National Lakeshore

It doesn't get much better than this—4 miles of trail through boreal forest perched on a ridgeline overlooking the greatest of the Great Lakes. Timeless.

Lake or river: Lake Superior
Photogenic factor: 5+
Distance: 3.6 miles out and back
Difficulty: Moderate with a few steep slopes
Hiking time: 90 minutes to 2 hours
Trail surface: Boardwalk and hard-packed dirt
Other trail users: None
Canine compatibility: Leashed pets allowed

Land status: National Park Service
Fees and permits: Daily vehicle permit required
Maps: Park service maps; USGS Port Wing
Trail contacts: Apostle Islands National Lakeshore, 415 Washington Ave., Bayfield 54814; (715) 779-3397; nps.gov/apis

Finding the trailhead: From Cornucopia, follow WI 13 north and east 3.8 miles to Meyers Road and turn left. The road ends in 0.3 mile at the trailhead and beach. **Trailhead GPS:** N46 88.303' / W91 04.764'

The Hike

Sculpted into labyrinthian designs by eons of howling wind and Lake Superior's thrashing waves, Wisconsin's Apostle Islands National Lakeshore is a siren song for those of adventuresome mind. Twelve miles of rugged and breathtakingly beautiful mainland shoreline includes bluffs, beaches, and the world-renowned sea caves.

The waterlogged caves are best experienced up close from the seat of a whisper-quiet kayak, or on foot in winter's icy grip. A wildly popular walking "trail" leads from Meyers Beach to the caves and what a sight to behold, with curtains of enormous icicles concealing entrances and bulbous blobs of hardened water clinging to the cliffs like slippery remoras. It's great fun exploring this magical place—put it on your bucket list.

Warmer seasons are all about hiking, and the Lakeshore Trail is a jewel. The first stretch of the hike follows a masterfully crafted plank boardwalk through resplendent boreal forest of maple, pine birch, and aspen, along with groundcover of huge ferns and mossy logs. The path is flat for the most part with several stream crossings in shallow ravines thrown in for a little challenge and adventure. These will be a bit slippery after rains so use caution and wear sturdy footwear for the best grippage.

A short spur trail a little over halfway in leads to a teaser overlook of the lake, Meyers Beach, and the squiggly mainland. This is a wildly popular destination for kayakers and it's common to see lots of them out there navigating the waters. A bit farther on you'll reach the first "official" sea cave overlook and 'tis a beauty. At trailside is a wooden fence surrounding the top of a 100-foot-deep gash in the weathered

The rugged sea cave cliffs.

Early section of the boardwalk trail.   *Bridge crossing on the trail.*

gray rock. A natural stone bridge connects the two sides, but the fence is there for a reason—it would be very bad to fall down in there.

There are good views into the depths by carefully peering over the edge, and you're likely to see a colorful kayak paddling in. The sea caves are of course best seen from a vessel at water level, and if you don't have one of your own, check out a rental or guided tour. Nonetheless, it is still outrageously beautiful from up here on top. The raggedy cliff is cloaked with grizzled pines, but ample openings provide otherworldly views of Lake Superior; in addition to canoes and kayaks, look for sailboats and giant ore freighters way out there. This is a fine place indeed to settle in for a mid-hike trail picnic and after that, more cave overlooks appear just a little farther down the trail. Way at the end is a sublime remote backcountry campsite. If you're of backpacking mind, don't miss this one.

From the first overlook, simply follow the same trail back to the trailhead. Along the way, reflect back on the Apostle Islands' fascinating history. Did you know traces of human history on the islands date to around 100 BC? In "more recent" times of the AD 950 era, Anishinaabe people migrated from the eastern United States following waterway trade routes in use for thousands of years and recorded the events on birch bark scrolls. Sometime around the 1400s, Ojibwa Indians established farming and mining practices during their time on these islands.

In another stroke of fascinating trivia, the Apostle Islands were not always islands. In fact, they were originally part of the mainland until glacial meltwater waves from the lake eroded the land in unfathomable ways to form today's island archipelago. The Apostle Islands name came from the Jesuit tradition of bestowing holy names to new places.

Apostle Islands National Lakeshore

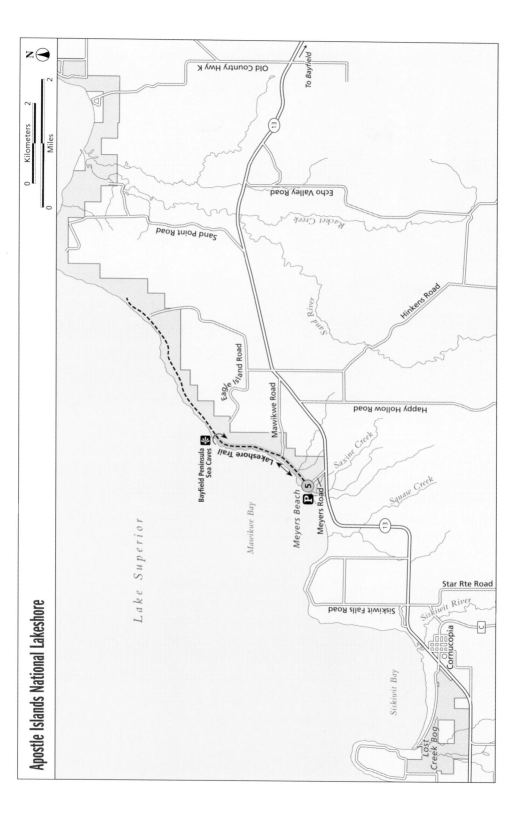

A kayaker explores a sea cave.

Miles and Directions

0.0 From the trailhead, hike into the woods on the double-wide plank boardwalk.

0.7 Cross a service trail and continue through the woods.

1.8 Arrive at the sea cave overlook. Return the same way.

3.6 Arrive back at the trailhead. (Note that several more cave overlooks are just a short distance farther on the trail.)

THE APOSTLE ISLANDS

The Apostle Islands (north and east of Bayfield Peninsula) are home to North America's largest concentrations of black bears, with many residing on Stockton, Sand, and Oak Islands. Bears are highly mobile, however, and can be found on nearly all of the islands. The Apostles also offer critical nesting habitat to gulls, double-crested cormorants, and great blue herons. In fact, Gull and Eagle Islands combine to host 80 percent of breeding herring gulls on Lake Superior's entire Wisconsin shore.

6 Brule Portage Trail

This longtime author favorite trail is thought to be the oldest in Wisconsin, used for centuries by Native Americans, explorers, missionaries, and later the intrepid voyageurs of the North Country. Follow their historical steps on this legendary route marking the headwaters of two mighty rivers.

Lake or river: Brule River and Upper St. Croix Lake
Photogenic factor: 5
Distance: 4.0 miles out and back
Difficulty: Moderate
Hiking time: About 2 hours
Trail surface: Dirt singletrack with scattered rocks
Other trail users: None

Canine compatibility: Leashed pets allowed
Land status: State forest
Fees and permits: None
Maps: State forest maps; USGS Solon Springs
Trail contacts: Brule River State Forest, 6250 S. Ranger Rd., Brule 54820; (715) 372-5678; dnr.wi.gov/topic/StateForests/BruleRiver/. North Country Trail Association, Brule St. Croix Chapter; northcountrytrail.org.

Finding the trailhead: From the village of Solon Springs, follow CR A northeast for 3.7 miles to the trailhead. Parking is available at the boat landing. **Trailhead GPS:** N46 37.975' / W91 7777.810'

The Hike

The Bois Brule River is a revered and storied waterway, with hundreds of years of tales to tell. The ancestors of the birch trees along the riverbanks provided inspiration—and raw materials—for the earliest canoes of the Chippewa. The intrepid *voyageurs* followed during the heady days of the fur trade. Close behind were headstrong miners and tireless lumbermen, plying the waters and surrounding forests in their trades.

Canoeists on the Brule today enjoy the same postcard scenery around every bend, including a few colossal white pines soaring skyward, providing ideal perch and nesting sites for bald eagles. The nearby Brule River Bog is an emerald-green incubator of primordial white cedar, spongy mosses, and dozens of rare plants like the Lapland buttercup. Still as the eye of a storm, the bog is bisected by 3,500 feet of boardwalk suspended above a fascinating wetland of soft peat soil and a thick upper layer of what is called "dense organic entanglement." It's spongy to the touch and amazingly regulates water flow of the river. Do not miss a life-list hike through this fairy-tale woods. Get there via a short side trip on the well-marked trail to St. Croix Creek. The bog trail starts just past the creek.

Like most of Wisconsin's dramatic geographical landscapes, the valleys of the Brule and St. Croix Rivers were carved by receding glaciers. Meltwater from ancient

Upper St. Croix Lake.

Lake Superior and nearby lands flowed through a newly formed divide, from which the two rivers flow today. The headwaters of each originate at a continental divide near the start of the bog trail. The spring-fed Brule flows north 44 miles to Lake Superior and the St. Croix flows first from its namesake lake, south to the confluence with the Mississippi, and onward to the Gulf of Mexico.

The portage trail, first formally recorded by French explorer Daniel Greysolon Sieur DuLhut, served as a critical link between Lake Superior and the Mississippi. A stone marker commemorating DuLhut rests along the trail, as well as other stones for explorers with names like Lesueur, Carver, and Schoolcraft. The path today shares its route with the North Country National Scenic Trail.

With all of this fascinating history at hand, begin the hike with a gradual climb into elegant forest of pine, maple, aspen, birch, and their relatives. The path quickly

THE RIVER OF PRESIDENTS

In addition to its extraordinary beauty, the Brule River is a world-class fishing stream. Lively trout and the area's sublime solitude attracted five US presidents to Cedar Island Lodge, a rustic retreat on an especially scenic bend in the river. Presidents Grant, Cleveland, Coolidge, Hoover, and Eisenhower spent time here relaxing on retreats from their demanding jobs. In fact, Coolidge enjoyed the "summer White House" so much he stayed nearly the entire summer of 1928, relaxing and occasionally tending to political matters. A high school in Superior, 30 miles away, was transformed into a presidential business hub and the school's library became Coolidge's temporary Oval Office.

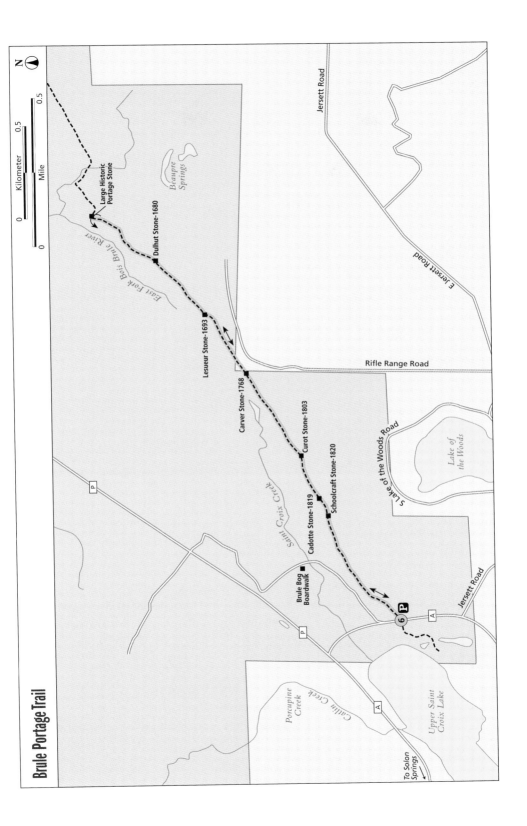

Brule Portage Trail

N

Kilometer
0   0.5

Mile
0   0.5

Porcupine Creek

Catlin Creek

Upper Saint Croix Lake

To Solon Springs

A

P

P

Brule Bog Boardwalk

Saint Croix Creek

Carver Stone-1768

Cadotte Stone-1819

Curot Stone-1803

Schoolcraft Stone-1820

Lesueur Stone-1693

East Fork Bois Brule River

Dulhut Stone-1680

Large Historic Portage Stone

Beaupre Springs

Rifle Range Road

S Lake of the Woods Road

Lake of the Woods

Jersett Road

E Jersett Road

Jersett Road

6
P

A

A peaceful section of the portage trail.

gains the top of the ridge, with occasional views of the shallow river valley. Evidence of a devastating hail storm in 2000 is still visible across the valley, where selective cutting and planting of seedlings was completed to help forest regeneration.

After a couple small undulations and a longer descent, the trail reaches the turnaround point at a spur trail leading to a viewing platform near the Brule River's earliest stretches. Check it out and then retrace your tracks to the trailhead. Bonus for backpackers: The Jersett Creek campsite is only another 2.5 miles farther on and author-recommended for heartbeat-quiet nights in the embrace of the forest.

Miles and Directions

0.0 From the trailhead, follow the North Country Trail blaze up the hill. Near the top is the Lucius Stone, the first commemorative explorer marker.

1.6 Right about here, just off-trail past the Lesueur Stone, is one-half (east fork) of the birth of the Bois Brule River. Hike another 0.4 mile to the Portage Stone and turnaround point.

4.0 Arrive at the trailhead.

7 Tomahawk Lake Trails

Choose from three loop options in this intimate small-town park, packed with rolling hills and resplendent North Country forest. Bonus points for trailhead access to the lake for post-hike refreshment.

Lake or river: Tomahawk Lake
Photogenic factor: 4
Distance: 1.6-mile loop, with 3.8- and 5.0-mile options
Difficulty: Moderate, with some hilly sections
Hiking time: 60 to 75 minutes
Trail surface: Hard-packed dirt and grassy section

Other trail users: None
Canine compatibility: Leashed pets allowed
Land status: Town of Barnes
Fees and permits: None
Maps: USGS Ellison Lake; town maps
Trail contacts: Town of Barnes, 3360 CR N, Barnes 54983; (715) 795-2782; barnes-wi.com

Finding the trailhead: From the Barnes Town Hall, follow Barnes Road north 0.5 mile to Ellison Lake Road and turn left. Go 0.5 mile to Moore Road and turn right. Follow Moore Road 1.2 miles to Park Road and turn left into the park. The trail starts adjacent to the shelter and boat launch.
Trailhead GPS: N46 36.693' / W91 51.181'

The Hike

In the late 1800s early settlers to northern Wisconsin began staking claim to new places to call home. George Barnes was among them, and he fancied the area around today's Eau Claire Lakes. Ol' George was a wise fella because this is indeed a very special place.

At the time of George's arrival, this was for the most part unsettled, wild country, populated mainly by scattered Chippewa Indian families and a woodsman or three. The land was blanketed with dense, old-growth forest and packed with all manner of wild critters, but Mr. Barnes had a hunch and established the area's first hotel, complemented with a general store and, of course, a saloon.

His vision proved clear and before long new settlers wandered in, eventually forming a little town around them, which took on its founder's name. In addition to his work running the town's main establishments, George was also the postmaster and mail carrier, traveling from Barnes to Iron River with a team of horses and carriage to retrieve his town's mail for delivery.

Since those heady days of discovery, challenge, and inspiration, a good majority of Wisconsin's north transformed into a wildly popular summer travel destination with vividly clear lakes, loon song, and an unspoken connection to your soul. Indeed, I share a kinship with this area's earliest residents with five generations of family heritage, and we are fiercely proud to be here.

The wide, woodsy trail.

High water at Tomahawk Lake's northern shore.

Speaking of lakes, the Eau Claire Chain comprises three big ones orbited by a supporting cast of smaller lakes with their own magic. The Upper, Middle, and Lower Eau Claire Lakes and friends host the headwaters of the Eau Claire River, which leisurely amble to the St. Croix River and then south to the Mississippi.

Just north of the big three lakes is Tomahawk Lake, about 130 acres shaped like its name and home to largemouth bass, panfish, and walleye. The little town park at the lake's north end is a base camp of sorts for outdoor pursuits and a source of community pride. Among stands of elegant forest are about 5 miles of squiggly trails wandering rolling hill and dale. An interpretive trail with accompanying signage is in the works and trees harvested for additional trail expansion are used for fish habitat in the lake as well as a fishing pier.

Start this hike traveling north from the trailhead, shortly passing the perch of the sledding hill. Hot tip: Don't miss this spot for whoop-it-up fun in the winter. Bring the kids and sleds and let 'er rip.

The trail is constructed wide for skiing and the tread is largely grassy, with streaks of dirt singletrack now and again. The entire first half of this loop takes in some of the prettiest of the woods, vibrant with oak, maple, red and white pine, and some

GIMME SHELTER

Snow lovers come hither! Those of the cross-country ski, snowshoe, and sledding mind now have a convenient base camp. A new, year-round park shelter sprouted here in 2019 and does duty as a warming hut, changing building, and safety shelter. The location is also available for community events and offers an outdoor well with fresh, icy-cold water in warm months and comfy wood heat when the snow falls.

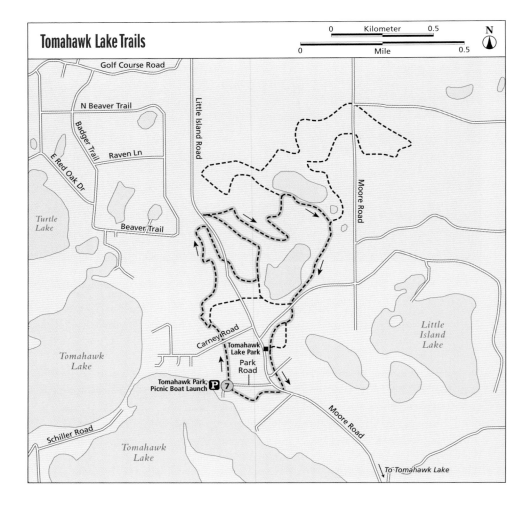

Tomahawk Lake Trails

Golf Course Road

N Beaver Trail

Badger Trail

E Red Oak Dr

Raven Ln

Little Island Road

Moore Road

Turtle Lake

Beaver Trail

Carney Road

Little Island Lake

Tomahawk Lake

Tomahawk Lake Park

Park Road

Tomahawk Park, Picnic Boat Launch

Schiller Road

Tomahawk Lake

Moore Road

To Tomahawk Lake

Norway pine. You'll enjoy flowing hills of varying steepness to keep things interesting, and on the eastern, back side of the loop, the terrain levels a bit on its homestretch to the trailhead.

Huge bonus: A lovely little swimming beach is conveniently located at trail's end for a refreshing conclusion to the hike.

Miles and Directions

0.0 Follow the blazes and signage north from the trailhead.

0.2 Turn left at this junction.

0.9 Turn right here for the short loop. (A left turn takes you on the two longer loop options.) Follow this section of the trail east about 600 feet.

1.0 Turn right here, hiking southbound.

1.6 Arrive back at the trailhead.

8 Green Lake Trail

Get off-the-grid solitude every step of the way on this short hike in the midst of hundreds of remote lakes steeped in area lore.

Lake or river: Green Lake
Photogenic factor: 4
Distance: 1.5-mile loop
Difficulty: Easy
Hiking time: About 45 minutes
Trail surface: Hard-packed dirt
Other trail users: None

Canine compatibility: Leashed pets allowed
Land status: County forest
Fees and permits: None
Maps: USGS North Green Lake
Trail contacts: Hayward Lakes Visitors & Convention Bureau, 15805 US 63, Hayward 55843; (715) 634-4801; haywardlakes.com

Finding the trailhead: From Stone Lake, follow CR BB south (becomes Ranch Road in 2 miles). At about 4.5 miles the road morphs again, this time to West Sissabagama Road. At 6.5 miles take the right split on North Green Lake Road and follow it south 1 mile to the trailhead on the left. **Trailhead GPS:** N45 74.337' / W91 51.581'

The Hike

Green Lake is a face among many in this heavily wooded and rolling section of Wisconsin, and it's blissfully remote, hence its appearance in this book. It's a treat to have places like this around us, and it doesn't get much better than Green Lake for big solitude. With its rolling terrain, barely there human population, stunning forest, and abundant wildlife, hikers can expect all kinds of seclusion and a tailor-made setting in which to reflect and revive.

LAKE COO DA RAY

The area around Big and Little Sissabagama Lakes was home to Chippewa Indian tribes for more than a century when the Lac Courte Oreilles Reservation was established in 1854. However, this land has seen a far richer history, hosting an array of tribes for well over 700 years. Everything the tribes needed was here and in plentiful supply—game, fish, blueberries, wild rice, and furs.

The Chippewa migrated to the present-day Lac Courte Oreilles area all the way from the Atlantic Coast to flee pressure from increasing numbers and volatility of various confrontations. Once known as Ottawa Lake, French fur traders renamed it Lac Courte Oreilles ("Lake Short Ears") for differences in the ears of Ojibwa who lived around the lake.

Quiet birch-lined trail.

For me, one of the best parts about hiking or any other outdoor pursuit is the palpable aura of the area's rich history and peace. Big and Little Sissabagama Lakes, just north of Green, are two of the state's most renowned. In fact, more than a few longtime locals, esteemed naturalists, DNR scientist types, and intermittent vaca-tioners will tell you that Little Sis is one of the finest examples of a quintessential

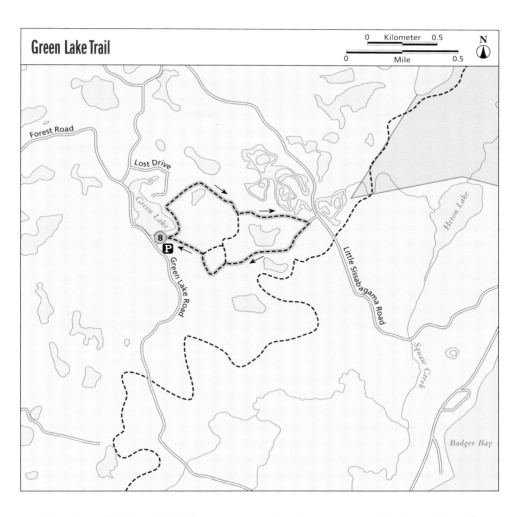

Green Lake Trail

0 — Kilometer — 0.5
0 — Mile — 0.5

N

Forest Road

Lost Drive

Green Lake

8

P

Green Lake Road

Little Sissabagama Road

Heron Lake

Squaw Creek

Badger Bay

Northwoods lake, with its diverse topography, clear waters, sandy shores, dense forest cover, historic cabins, and vibrant wildlife. That's an audacious claim considering a state packed with life-list locales, but I'm sure you'll agree.

And I can't get enough of the proud history here. Up until the late 1800s, Chippewa, Menominee, Oneida, Potawatomi, and Winnebago tribes lived and flourished in this area of abundant wildlife and forests offering protection and resources. Loggers, trappers, and explorers followed, traveling and trading exclusively by waterways, and Native American language remains prominent in Wisconsin. The Sissabagama name we see today can be translated to "Lake of Many Bays."

Start this hike by circling Green Lake's southeastern shore, with great views of the water through breaks in the stands of birch and maple. The path passes a backcountry campsite perched on a hill above the lake. It's a great place to pitch a tent, especially in the fall when colors are a'blazin'. Across the top side of the loop, the path continues

Secluded Green Lake from the trail.

through resplendent forest of pine, birch, maple, ash, tamarack, and more on a rolling track to the north shore of a cupcake-shaped lake way out there.

Pass the eastern trailhead and start a longer climb to a nice view of another backwoods lake, and then take on a few more rollers before a gentle descent to the trailhead.

Since you're in the area, head up to the Stone Lake Wetland Park, a fascinating 17 acres of wetland with walking trails, a 600-foot-long boardwalk, covered bridge, and gazebo overlooking the lake. Trails are open in winter to skiing and snowshoeing too.

Miles and Directions

0.0 From the trailhead, hike left and north in a clockwise direction.

0.5 Turn left at this junction.

0.8 Pass the east trailhead and turn back southwest.

1.2 Turn left here, following outer perimeter of the trail.

1.5 Arrive back at the trailhead.

9 Hayward Recreational Forest

Hayward buzzes with all manner of activity in the summer months, but you can get wilderness-like peace and quiet in the town's namesake getaway forest.

Lake or river: Konieczny Lake
Photogenic factor: 4
Distance: 2.8-mile loop
Difficulty: Easy to moderate
Hiking time: About 1 hour
Trail surface: Short section of gravel at start, then mowed grass
Other trail users: None

Canine compatibility: Leashed pets allowed
Land status: Town of Hayward
Fees and permits: None
Maps: USGS Stanberry East
Trail contacts: Hayward Lakes Visitors & Convention Bureau, 15805 US 63, Hayward 55843; (715) 634-4801; haywardlakes.com

Finding the trailhead: From US 63 at the south side of Hayward, follow Greenwood Lane north 0.8 mile to County Hill Road. Turn left and follow County Hill west 1.8 miles to the forest area entrance. It's the next driveway past the gravel pit. Only one little sign currently stands and faces west so remember to turn after the gravel pit. **Trailhead GPS:** N46 01 078' / W91 53.476'

The Hike

Opened for business back in 2011, this relatively young outdoor rec area boasts 160 acres of mildly undulating to hilly terrain overlaid with a dense population of white and red pine, oak, maple, aspen, birch, and a variety of other species I couldn't identify. The understory is a cavalcade of shrubbery and ferns common to the north, as well as a bazillion wood ticks. The paths are mowed, but be aware and check thoroughly after the hike for those little buggers.

Did I mention mosquitoes? Stop moving for more than, say, 15 seconds and they will eat you. Dry periods are typically better (less perilous), but expect the hordes all summer and bring bug repellent and appropriate clothing. I brought neither the day I hiked here and, well, I hiked fast. One other nugget to remember is the forest is closed to hiking during the annual gun deer-hunting season, from the Saturday before Thanksgiving to the Sunday after.

Okay, let's hike. The trails were designed for cross-country skiing and hence are very wide. Plenty of room to walk hand in hand or chase your lively child around. The first stretch of trail leading to the south parking area and warming house is on gravel, but the remaining mileage is all mowed grass. This trail system is made of a collection of loops and ancillary trails for whatever suits your mood. Today, shoot for the start of the Green Trail southeast of the warming house. This section tracks through plenty o' pines and the deciduous species mentioned above. The path undulates a little, with one gradual rise and a short, punchy climb. Pass by stands of aspen

A small tamarack stand at the lake's southern shore.

and birch to the Orange Trail and head southwest to Konieczny Lake, named for the area's original landowners.

I chose this hike for its easy access from town, scenic factor, and this little, hidden lake. The lake isn't a calendar-shot candidate, but it's one of those way-out-there, all-natural places that we love so much in these parts of the state. Lily pads carpet some areas of the surface and in late summer bloom with the white accents of their puffball flowers. Ancient deadfall logs float here and there, and there is almost always some form of wildlife visiting the lake. Look for ducks, herons, deer, turtles, and mosquitoes. A bench perched on the shore is great for reflection time in the fall when the bugs are gone.

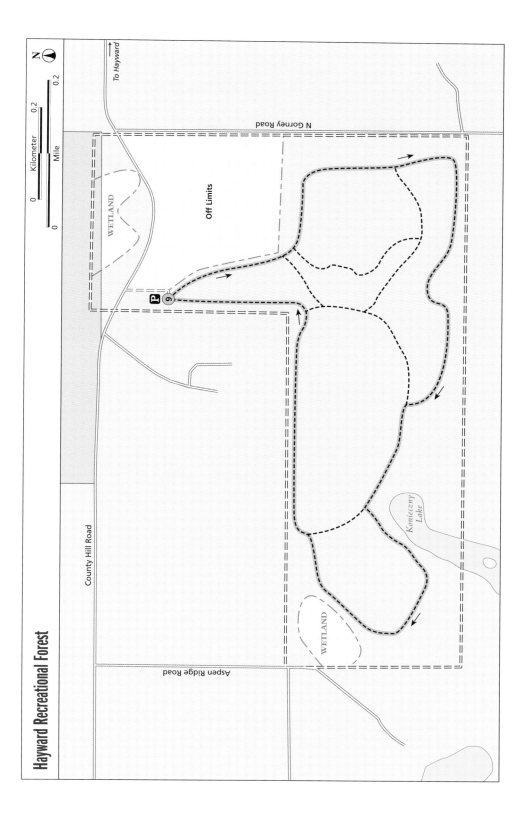

Hayward Recreational Forest

A ship's prow log among blooming lily pads.

The top part of the loop heads arrow-straight back to the final stretch north to the trailhead. Don't forget to come back in winter for sublime XC skiing and snowshoeing.

Miles and Directions

0.0 Head south from the trailhead and follow the Green Trail to the left.

0.8 Keep heading straight on the Yellow Trail.

1.3 Turn left on the Blue Trail.

1.5 Turn left on the Orange Trail.

2.0 Veer left/straight on the Blue Trail.

2.8 Arrive back at the trailhead.

THE KISSICK ALKALINE BOG

Wisconsin is loaded with ecological gems and one of the most fascinating is the Kissick Alkaline Bog State Natural Area. This area features a 10-acre wilderness lake surrounded by an enormous and rare quaking bog mat and wet forest. This special place is home to no fewer than fourteen native orchid species, narrow-leaved sundew, pitcher plant, boreal sedge, and bog-rosemary. Black spruce and tamarack forest dominates the fringe of the bog, along with white cedar and cattails. The alkaline-to-acid variation inspires the bog's incredible diversity.

10 Glacier Trail–Chequamegon-Nicolet National Forest

Shuh-WAH-muh-guhn. Up in these parts, that name is synonymous with more than *1.5 million* acres of sublime North Country forest and a lifetime of unforgettable hiking trails. This next pair shows off some of the forest's finest.

Lake or river: Rock Lake
Photogenic factor: 4+
Distance: 1.6 miles out and back to Rock Lake on Glacier Trail segment; 4.0-mile loop on Rock Lake and Emerson Lake Trails
Difficulty: Easy to moderate, with some hilly sections on the Rock Lake loop
Hiking time: About 45 minutes for Glacier Trail; 2-3 hours for Rock Lake loop
Trail surface: Hard-packed dirt singletrack

Other trail users: None
Canine compatibility: Leashed pets allowed
Land status: Chequamegon-Nicolet National Forest
Fees and permits: None
Maps: CAMBA trail maps; USGS Lake Tahkodah
Trail contacts: Chequamegon-Nicolet National Forest, 500 Hansen Rd., Rhinelander 54501; (715) 362-1300; fs.usda.gov/cnnf

Finding the trailhead: From Cable, drive 7.9 miles east on CR M to Rock Lake Road (FR 207). Turn right and head south 1.9 miles to the Glacier Trail junction parking area.
Trailhead GPS: N46 17.316' / W91 13.193'

The Hike

I've been fortunate to hike and camp all around the country, and home state bias aside, the Chequamegon shares top billing with the very best. There are nowhere near enough superlatives to do this place justice. Indeed, it's nothing short of heaven on earth for hikers and backpackers, with more than 800 miles of trails strewn all over the forest like an Etch A Sketch drawing gone wild.

The biggest problem I have every time I set foot in these woods is leaving them, and this area in the vicinity of Rock and Wilson Lakes is testament to why. The brilliant old-growth forest here was logged to oblivion in the early 1930s and only a few remnant and very small stands of the majestic hemlock and white and red pine remain. However, the CCC in their tireless ways played a big part in reforesting the area into the vibrant second-growth lands we see today, embellished with splotches of clear-water lakes and squiggly lines of rivers and streams noodling about.

This short hike with an optional (and nearly irresistible) bonus loop heads into the Rock Lake SNA and the shores of its namesake lake. The skinny path follows a gently rolling course through elegant pine-hardwood forest with nary another soul to be found. With every footstep you'll sing praise to the vision and unceasing dedication of everyone involved with the Chequamegon Area Mountain Bike Association

Trailside birch in fall. GETTY/NORTHWOODSPHOTO

(CAMBA). This intrepid group of fat-tire enthusiasts, volunteers, and local businesses has seamlessly morphed with local and federal agencies to create one of the premier mountain-bike destinations in the country. Over 300 miles of trails are mapped and marked, awaiting hikers, bikers, and skiers. See the sidebar for more scoop.

This hike to Rock Lake sets off from the Glacier Trailhead on Rock Lake Road. Follow the path up and over a small ridge into woods heavy with maple and aspen.

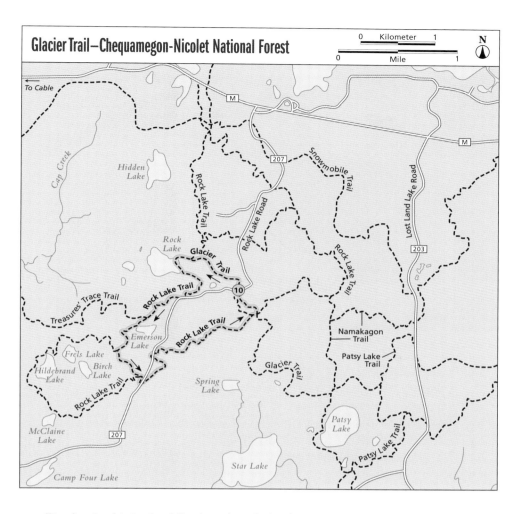

Glacier Trail–Chequamegon-Nicolet National Forest

(Don't miss this in the fall, when the whole place is blazin' with orange and yellow.) Merge with the Rock Lake Trail and wander past big white pines to the ridge above Rock Lake's eastern shore. A short way south leads to a campsite path down to the water for sweet views across the lake. From here, return the same way or continue southbound on the Rock Lake Trail for the long loop, passing Emerson Lake and curving back northeast to the Glacier Trail.

Miles and Directions

0.0 Head up the hill from the trailhead.

0.6 At the junction with Rock Lake Trail, keep hiking westbound.

0.8 Arrive at Rock Lake. The short route returns from here.

1.6 Arrive at the trailhead.

Long loop directions from Rock Lake:

A spruce grouse along the trail. GETTY/BOOKGUY

0.8 Continue south on Rock Lake Trail.

1.2 At the junction with Treasures' Trace Trail, keep on straight ahead.

1.7 At the junction with Hildebrand Lake Loop, turn left on Emerson Lake Cutoff.

2.0 At the junction with connector trail to Rock Lake Road, turn left and follow the connector to the road. Rock Lake Trail continues across the road.

3.7 At the junction with Glacier Trail, turn left.

4.0 Arrive at the trailhead.

CAMBA RIDES STRONG

Born in 1992 at a casual meeting of local outdoors junkies, the Chequamegon Area Mountain Bike Association today boasts a trail system with over 300 miles of marked paths exploring rolling, glaciated terrain accented with secluded lakes and streams, high ridges, wetlands, eskers, and bogs. Split into six clusters from Hayward to Iron River, the trails are impeccably maintained, with every notable intersection and trailhead marked with CAMBA's blue logo signs and "You Are Here" map kiosks to ease directional woes. Trails are out there for all abilities, from cruises along abandoned logging roads to long and technical roller-coaster routes and a long-line singletrack stretch from Cable all the way to Hayward. Stay tuned in to their cambatrails.org website, where there's always something great happening with races, events, and trail updates.

11 Wilson Lake Trail—Chequamegon-Nicolet National Forest

The backpacking campsites at Wilson Lake are known as some of Wisconsin's most remote. This short hike to the lake's north shore backs up that claim—heartbeat quiet save for loon song and bullfrogs.

Lake or river: Wilson Lake
Photogenic factor: 4
Distance: 2.0 miles out and back
Difficulty: Easy
Hiking time: About 45 minutes
Trail surface: Hard-packed dirt path
Other trail users: None
Canine compatibility: Leashed pets allowed

Land status: Chequamegon-Nicolet National Forest
Fees and permits: None
Maps: CAMBA trail maps; USGS Namekagon Lake
Trail contacts: Chequamegon-Nicolet National Forest, 500 Hansen Rd., Rhinelander 54501; (715) 362-1300; fs.usda.gov/cnnf

Finding the trailhead: From Cable, drive 9.5 miles east on CR M to Lost Land Lake Road (FR 203). Turn right and head south 3.2 miles to FR 206. Turn right and go southwest 1 mile to the Wilson Lake Trailhead. **Trailhead GPS:** N46 14.038' / W91 11.613'

The Hike

"Think of our life in nature—daily to be shown matter, to come in contact with it—rocks, trees, wind on our cheeks! *Contact! Contact! Who* are we? *Where* are we?"

If I had to choose one of the many inspiring Thoreau quotes, this would be it. *Contact.* I always feel best when I can lay my hand on a bed of velvety-smooth moss, or sit on an old log and breathe in the scents and spirit of a noble white pine, or walk with the peace of a forest. It's good to be out there, and this short hike to Wilson Lake is elixir for the soul.

Entirely within the Wilson Lake State Natural Area, the path starts wide from the trailhead, heading westbound on the Patsy Lake Trail into a similarly spellbinding forest as on the Rock Lake hike. The Wilson Lake SNA boasts a mosaic of sedge meadow ecosystems and northern dry-mesic forests. Sphagnum grass and sedge

WHERE DID THE NEEDLES GO?

If you see a stand of "naked" conifers, don't be alarmed. Those are tamaracks, also known as larch. This hardy tree is one of only a few coniferous species with needles that turn yellow and drop in the fall. Tamaracks are commonly found in bogs or sedge mats around lakes and its wood was used by Native Americans to make snowshoes.

Sunrise on the lake. GETTY/PAUL SCHMIDT

species dominate here and blend with lake and stream riparian areas. Beyond the sedges are second-growth white and red pine born of past fire events and small stands of old-growth closer to nearby Star Lake.

After about a third of a mile, the junction with the Wilson Lake Trail appears, while the Patsy trail goes north. Turn left here and trace along a few gentle undulations in a unique blend of meadows and second-growth ecosystems thriving among glacial eskers. Cattail marshes appear here and there, as well as blueberry, big laurel, and the beauteous dragon's-mouth orchid, a special-concern plant here in Wisconsin. (That means it lives in a restricted range and populations are susceptible to harm.)

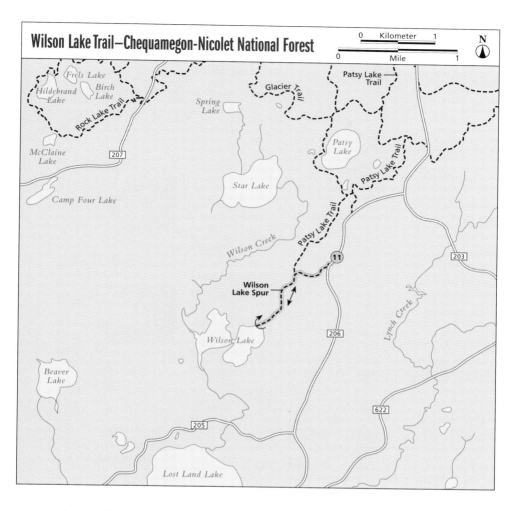

Plenty of stately white and red pine line the trail, and before you know it, Wilson Lake shows itself. The trail ends at one of two backpack campsites, with shoreside views of this gorgeous bog lake filled with bass, perch, bluegill, and others of that ilk. In the fall the lake is fringed with the golden glow of tamarack. It's all kinds of quiet here and one of Wisconsin's best spots to throw down a tent and channel your inner Thoreau.

Miles and Directions

0.0 Hike west from the trailhead.

0.3 At the junction with Wilson Lake Trail, veer left.

1.0 Arrive at Wilson Lake. Return to the trailhead the same way you came.

2.0 Arrive at the trailhead.

12 Rainbow Lake Wilderness—North Country Trail

Rainbow Lakes is one of our country's earliest wilderness areas and today includes over 6,500 acres and a legendary wolf pack. This short hike touches the heart of the wilderness on the epic North Country Trail.

Lake or river: Wishbone and Reynard Lakes
Photogenic factor: 5
Distance: 2.3 miles one-way or 4.6 miles out and back
Difficulty: Easy to moderate
Hiking time: About 2 hours one-way
Trail surface: Hard-packed dirt path with scattered rocks and roots
Other trail users: None

Canine compatibility: Leashed pets allowed
Land status: National Park Service
Fees and permits: None
Maps: North Country Trail maps; USGS Drummond, USGS Delta
Trail contacts: North Country Trail Association, 229 E. Main St., Lowell, MI 49331; (866) HIKE-NCT; northcountrytrail.org

Finding the trailhead: From US 63 in Drummond, follow Delta-Drummond Road 3.9 miles north to Reynard Lake Road. Turn left and follow the road 0.8 mile to the trailhead.
Trailhead GPS: N46 38.863' / W91 28.495'

The Hike

Every time I'm out here, the same thing happens. I can't decide which way to go. It's beautiful that way and enchanting the other way. What to do? The North Country Trail is a highlight reel of life-list hiking, and its trailheads are like a conundrum of magnetic poles luring our boots in opposite directions of wilderness grace. It's okay, though, because we win either way.

THE LONG WALK

Long-distance hikers are a unique breed, wearing out the soles of their boots like long-haul Peterbilts shedding tread on a sunbaked Arizona interstate. The endurance crowd can channel their inner trucker on the North Country National Scenic Trail, covering seven states and 4,600 miles. Established in 1980, with origins long before, the NCT is the country's longest continuous trail, passing through daydream-worthy scenery all the while. The trail is named for the natural splendor of Wisconsin's Chequamegon-Nicolet National Forest.

Rainbow Lake Wilderness portal at the trailhead.

Rainbow Lake Wilderness was designated as such in 1975 and is known today for its resident timber wolf pack. Vilified and killed off by—what else?—human meddling like bounties and other despicable means, wolf numbers plummeted to just 200 in the 1920s. The last documented wolf was hit by a car in 1958, and with that one sickening blow of a fender, they were gone.

Neighboring forests in Minnesota harbored a scattering of wolf holdouts, which at the time was the only established population in the United States outside of Alaska. But in the early to mid-1970s, wolves began to reappear in Wisconsin. There was no complex, expensive, controversial reintroduction event—the wolves simply walked back in to reclaim their place. It happened slowly at first; a random sighting one day

Rainbow Lake Wilderness—North Country Trail

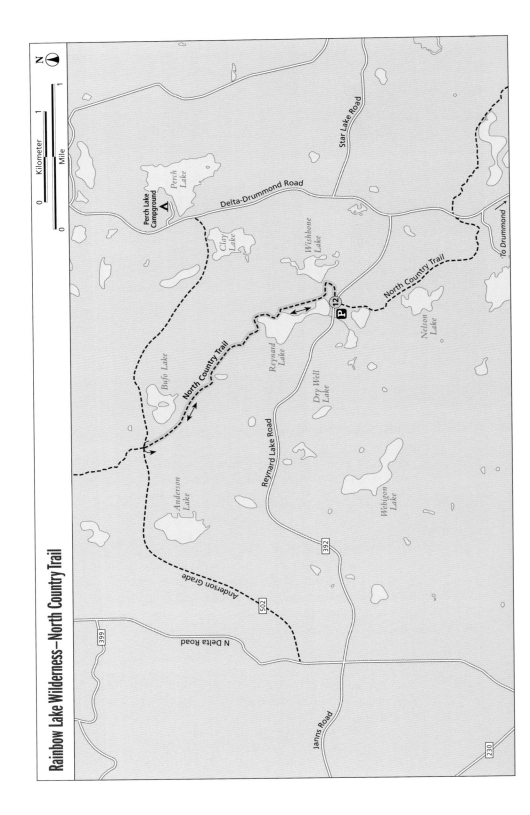

Reynard Lake through the trees.

or report to a forest office the next. Gradually their populations increased, and today we share our lands with nearly 1,000 of these regal beasts. The evocative wail of their call echoing in the woods on a coal-black night is the purest of song.

Along with wonderfully wild critters, this wilderness also features unique reminders of the area's non-wilderness past. In the 1900s logging scourge, narrow-gauge railroads were used to haul felled trees to mills, and while the tracks are long gone today, the gentle grades make ideal hiking routes. The NCT follows or passes near some of these historic rail lines, including the Anderson Grade on this hike.

From the trailhead, hike past the southwest shore of Wishbone Lake (Insider tip: this is a postcard-perfect place to launch a canoe) and then northbound along Reynard Lake's eastern shore, with extra-scenic views at both. Mosey through decadent hardwood forest to intermittent views of heart-shaped Bufo Lake before arriving at the junction with FR 502 (Anderson Grade). Decision time again but in a good way because the NCT makes it easy to keep right on hiking. For this chapter's "official" route, turn around here and head back. If you brought a tent, Anderson Lake sports a primo campsite just 1 mile west on the grade. Trek 3 miles north of the FR 502 turnaround past Rainbow Lake to the Delta Lookout Tower. An access road from the tower leads back toward "civilization." Or wander 2 miles south from the Reynard Lake trailhead to a parking turnout on Delta-Drummond Road.

Miles and Directions

0.0 From the trailhead, hike north around the edge of the lower bulb of Reynard Lake and loop past its northern nose on a northwesterly track.

1.8 Skirt the western shore of Bufo Lake.

2.3 At the junction with FR 502 (Anderson Grade), retrace your tracks back to Reynard Lake.

4.6 Arrive at the trailhead.

13 Porcupine Lake Wilderness—North Country Trail

Make a loop with the NCT on this short hike in the Porcupine Wilderness, and score a life-list campsite for an optional overnighter.

Lake or river: Porcupine Lake and Eighteen-mile Creek Springs
Photogenic factor: 5
Distance: 3.0-mile loop (with 4 optional bonus miles)
Difficulty: Easy to moderate
Hiking time: About 90 minutes
Trail surface: Hard-packed dirt path with scattered rocks and roots

Other trail users: None
Canine compatibility: Leashed pets allowed
Land status: National Park Service
Fees and permits: None
Maps: North Country Trail maps; USGS Diamond Lake
Trail contacts: North Country Trail Association, 229 E. Main St., Lowell, MI 49331; (866) HIKE-NCT; northcountrytrail.org

Finding the trailhead: From US 63 in Drummond, follow North Lake Owen Drive 5.3 miles south to Porcupine Lake Road and turn left. Head east 1.3 miles to the trailhead.
Trailhead GPS: N46 29.645' / W91 15.917'

The Hike

I like wandering in this part of the Porcupine Wilderness. The North Country Trail is extra squiggly, it's all kinds of remote out here, and the Porky is home to a wolf pack just like its wilderness neighbor to the north. Keep an eye out for their tracks on the trails, especially in winter—there's something very special about knowing you're not alone out here.

But it feels alone, and that's a good thing. From the Porcupine Lake area, the NCT takes hikers on a many-mile stretch through some of Wisconsin's most remote lands, passing through forest packed with the likes of maple, birch, aspen, pine, hemlock, and cedar. If you're of fishing mind, Porcupine Lake teems with panfish, bluegills, and trout.

COMPANY TOWN

Attracted by immense stands of white and Norway pine in the late 1800s, the Rust-Owen Lumber Company eyed northern Wisconsin as a fine place to build a sawmill. Crew leader Frank Drummond supervised construction of the mill, shack houses, barns, and a company store, all owned by the lumber company. The "town" was later named after Frank Drummond.

Early trail section through the pines.

Porcupine Creek.

Log bridge crossing Porcupine Creek.

Start this loop at the wilderness trailhead along Porcupine Lake Road. Walk into the woods and hike along Porcupine Creek, a gorgeous little stream flowing clear and clean from its namesake lake out toward Lake Superior. At the junction with

Porcupine Lake Wilderness—North Country Trail

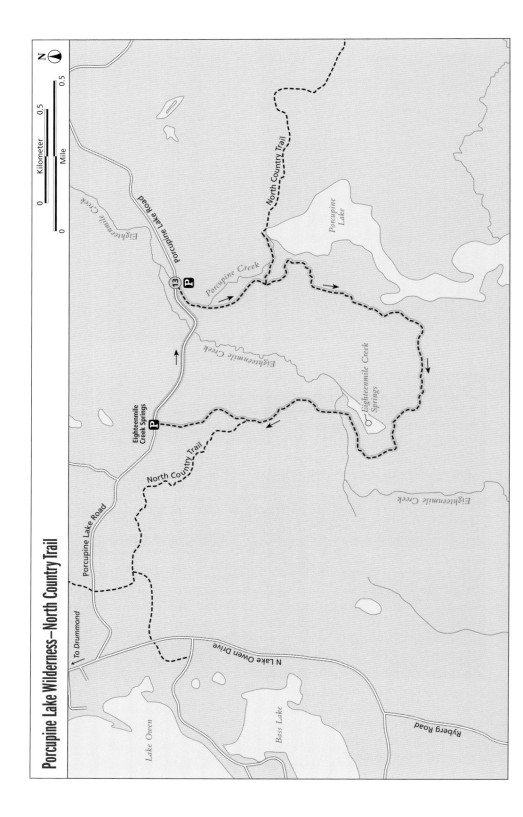

the NCT proper, take a left for a quick side trip to great views of the lake and then backtrack to the junction.

The trail gently rolls through resplendent forest with sometime views of Porcupine Lake to the east. In a short while you'll curve gradually to the west and up to a ridgeline flanking the southern shore of Eighteenmile Creek Springs, in essence a large, elongated pond feeding into Eighteenmile Creek. A short descent drops to a bridge over the creek, and after a couple of easygoing hills through stands of pine, you will meet the junction with the spur trail heading north to the road, while the NCT continues westbound.

At Porcupine Lake Road, you'll have to hoof it just shy of a half mile, but it's downhill on soft gravel back to the trailhead. Want more miles? Switch it up and start this hike at the spur trail turnout/trailhead on Porcupine Lake Road. Hike south and loop back up to the north side of Porcupine Lake and then follow the trail into a 4-mile stretch of heartbeat-quiet wilderness to the County D trailhead. Have a buddy pick you up or make a day of it and hike back to Porky's splendiferous lakeside campsites to spend the night.

Miles and Directions

0.0 From the trailhead, hike southbound on the generally flat trail through the woods.

0.3 At the junction with the NCT proper, go right to a gradual climb to a ridge with intermittent views of Porcupine Lake through the trees. *Trail note:* Do not miss the 0.3-mile side trip to the north end of the lake and the best views of the entire loop. Just go left at this junction to the shore and then back to finish the loop.

1.4 Follow the trail to the top of a high ridge above Eighteenmile Creek Springs.

1.8 Cross Eighteenmile Creek.

2.2 At the junction with the spur trail north, turn right.

2.5 At the junction with Porcupine Lake Road. Turn right and follow the dirt road back to the trailhead.

3.0 Arrive at the trailhead.

14 Copper Falls State Park—Doughboys Trail

Score a waterfall twofer and otherworldly North Country scenery on this life-list hike in the midst of deep river gorges, lively rivers, and stately forest.

Lake or river: Tyler Forks and Bad Rivers
Photogenic factor: 5
Distance: 2.3-mile loop (including spur to observation tower)
Difficulty: Easy to moderate
Hiking time: About 90 minutes
Trail surface: Hard-packed dirt path with scattered rocks and roots
Other trail users: None

Canine compatibility: Leashed pets allowed
Land status: State park
Fees and permits: Vehicle pass required
Maps: State park maps; USGS Mellen, USGS High Bridge
Trail contacts: Copper Falls State Park, 36764 Copper Falls Rd., Mellen 54546; (715) 274-5123; dnr.wi.gov/topic/parks/name/copperfalls/

Finding the trailhead: From Mellen, follow WI 13 north 0.5 mile to WI 169 and continue 1.7 miles to the park entrance. Follow the park road to the picnic area parking area and trailhead.
Trailhead GPS: N46 37.134' / W90 64.311'

The Hike

Another of my go-to favorites for adventure and breathtaking scenery, this popular state park sports two calendar-shot waterfalls way down in deep, rocky gorges on an exhilarating loop trail. North Country rugged mixed with old-time charm fills the air every step of the way. The picnic area and main grounds near the trailhead are

Bridge crossing over Bad River. DENICE BREAUX

Copper Falls from the trail. DENICE BREAUX

dotted with log buildings masterfully created by Civilian Conservation Corps members in the 1930s, surrounded by rich forests of hemlock, pine, sugar maple, birch, and basswood. Within the woods are dozens of wildlife species including tiger swallowtail butterflies, frogs, deer, pileated woodpeckers, and loons.

The history of this special place is equally intriguing and evident all along the hike in a fascinating blend of geologic artistry and copper-mining tradition. After enormous flows of lava oozed from the earth and layer upon layer of various types of rock formed on the land, the Bad River was born and has spent the past untold millions of years carving its way toward Lake Superior. Today we are treated to the result of the river's efforts in the 100-foot-deep gorge of Brownstone Falls.

A very long time after the gorge took shape, early Native Americans followed receding glaciers north, and later tribes, called Copper Culture Indians, established areas of copper mining. European settlers made valiant attempts to continue the pursuit of copper but with little success.

Start this fun hike at the parking area and immediately cross a short footbridge over the Bad River. At the top of a gradual rise is the junction with the trail to the observation tower. Lots of stairs climb the steep ridge and a few more take you to the top of the tower for beauteous views of the forest unfurling in all directions. Can you see Lake Superior way out there to the north? Head back to the river junction to continue the hike.

A wide, manicured stretch of trail leads to an overlook of Copper Falls, all told dropping about 29 feet in a collection of mini waterfalls flowing over jumbles of boulders. From here, the trail rises to another overlook with stellar views of Brownstone Falls shinnying through 100 feet of sandstone and black shale. Continue hiking along the ridge above the steep walls of Devil's Gate to a flight of stone steps descending to the river. This is a great spot to wander on sandbars and get up close to the river (during times of cooperative water levels).

Follow the bridge over the river and turn back eastbound, climbing back up to the top of the northern ridge and past the junction with the North Country Trail's arrival to the park's main attractions. A little farther on is a short spur trail leading to yet another overlook above the river, this time with great views of the confluence of the Tyler Forks River's confluence with the Bad, Brownstone Falls, and the

HISTORIC PEDIGREE

In November of 1935 Company D-692 of the Civilian Conservation Corps moved into Camp Copper Falls. The 164-strong company was made of carpenters, masons, furniture makers, and blacksmiths. In the ensuing two years, the skilled company built the park's recreational lodge, which included a granite fireplace along with log-inspired benches and tables. And that was just the beginning—the crew also built a pump house, water reservoirs, and the soaring observation tower and ran water and telephone lines. Some crew members were charged with clearing areas for visitor parking and picnicking, as well as space for camping. With ten contributing properties constructed by the Civilian Conservation Corps, Copper Falls State Park is listed on the National Register of Historic Places.

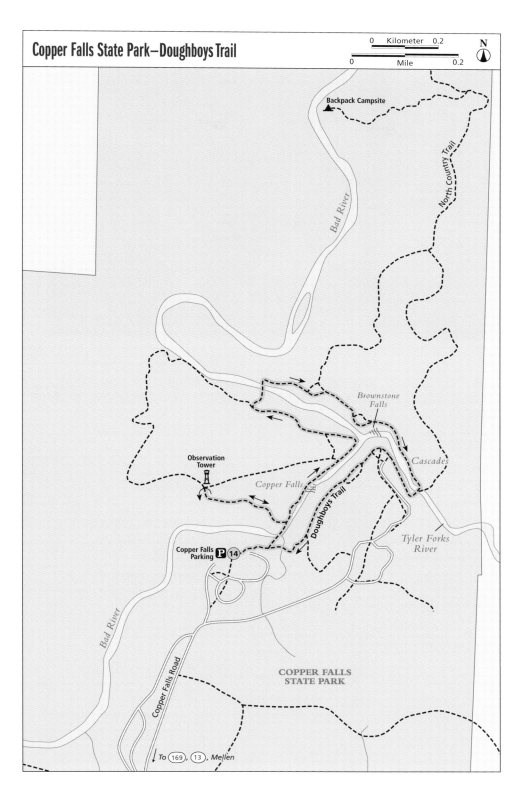

Copper Falls State Park–Doughboys Trail

0   Kilometer   0.2

0   Mile   0.2

N

Backpack Campsite

Bad River

North Country Trail

Brownstone Falls

Cascades

Observation Tower

Copper Falls

Doughboys Trail

Tyler Forks River

Copper Falls Parking

P 14

Bad River

Copper Falls Road

COPPER FALLS STATE PARK

To 169, 13, Mellen

Steep stairs on the trail. DENICE BREAUX

Tyler Forks Cascades. Keep hiking along the river to a bridge just upstream from the cascades, and loop back past a couple more overlooks on the homestretch to the trailhead.

Miles and Directions

0.0 Set off from the trailhead and cross the bridge.

0.1 At the junction with the observation-tower trail, turn left for great views.

0.3 Reach the tower, climb it, and retrace your tracks to the river.

0.5 Back at the river, follow the trail to the Copper Falls overlook and onward up the ridge.

0.7 At the overlook above Brownstone Falls, follow the path west along the ridge.

0.9 Bridge crossing over the Bad River.

1.2 Pass the junction with the North Country Trail. (Doughboys Trail shares ground with the NCT from here.)

1.3 This is the spur trail to river overlook.

1.5 A bridge crosses over the Tyler Forks River.

2.3 Arrive back at the trailhead.

15 Penokee Range—North Country Trail

This hike samples a wilder stretch of the NCT, with elevated views, verdant North-woods forest, and a pair of choice backcountry campsites.

Lake or river: Upson Lake
Photogenic factor: 5
Distance: 6.2 miles out and back
Difficulty: Moderate to difficult
Hiking time: 3+ hours
Trail surface: Hard-packed dirt
Other trail users: None
Canine compatibility: Leashed pets allowed

Land status: National Park Service
Fees and permits: None
Maps: North Country Trail maps; USGS Ironwood, MI
Trail contacts: North Country Trail Association, 229 E. Main St., Lowell, MI 49331; (866) HIKE-NCT; northcountrytrail.org

Finding the trailhead: From the village of Upson, follow WI 77 west 0.5 mile to Upson Lake Road and turn right. Head north 2.2 miles to Upson Lake. An unmaintained track loops 0.6 mile to the far southwest edge of the lake and the start of the NCT proper. Drive the track if your vehicle is up for it or hike from the end of Upson Lake Road. **Trailhead GPS:** N46 38.810' / W90 44.354'

The Hike

The Alps of Wisconsin? Yep, if you were around 500 million to 600 million years ago (give or take a few), this was the place to be for world-class mountaineering and gnarly skiing. The 80-mile-long Penokee Range (also called by its Ojibwa name, Gogebic Range) is one of the world's oldest, predating animal life on land. These hills once soared to more than 10,000 feet, with snow-covered summits and deep, verdant valleys, and the ridges of the Penokee are still among the highest in Wisconsin, rising about 800 feet above Lake Superior's surface.

Two hundred million years of erosion sculpted what we see today, accompanied by glacial artistry that left behind a handful of lakes and spruce-tamarack bogs. This is a very special place indeed, filled with rich forests of birch, aspen, and maple mingling with balsam fir, white pine, cedar, spruce, tamarack, and cedar. Bogs and grasslands border the higher hills, and animal life like you saw in the wilderness areas to the west settle here in abundance.

The late 1800s attracted thousands of immigrants to the range's rich veins of iron ore. Finnish, Austrian, Swedish, French-Canadian, and other families swarmed into the area and created small towns and communities. Mined iron was shipped by rail from here to Ashland and then on to shipping freighters bound for other Great Lakes ports. The boom continued into the 1920s and this area provided much of the nation's iron until the Great Depression put a damper on things. All told, roughly 325 million tons of iron ore were extracted via very deep underground shaft mines.

Upson Lake with a background of green. DENICE BREAUX

After recovering from the ravages of mining, rampant clear-cutting then took its toll on the state's noble old-growth forests. The land once again recovered, and today the Penokee Range hosts a vibrant outdoors-focused tourism industry that includes hunting and fishing, mountain biking, snowmobiling, and, of course, hiking.

This is a spectacular section of the North Country Trail and perfect for making it a long out-and-back day hike, or bring a tent and spend the night at the Gold Mine West or Wren Falls campsites for some of the NCT's best backcountry camping. Another don't-miss bonus is a side trip to Corrigan's Lookout. A short, 0.25-mile trail leads to grand vistas of Lake Superior, the Gogebic/Penokee Range, Upson Lake, and beyond.

Waterfalls and rock balcony overlooks are regular features of this range, and best of all, you're unlikely to see another soul out here. Instead, look for whitetail deer, ruffed grouse, pileated woodpeckers, dozens of songbird species, and black bears that roam these woods too.

From the trailhead, skirt the southern tip of a high ridgeline and curve along its flanking cirque-like contour. The path then follows a moderate ascent to the top of the ridge on its way through woods heavy with deciduous species on a generally level course to the junction with Casey Sag Road. Cross the road and follow the base of a

Penokee Range—North Country Trail

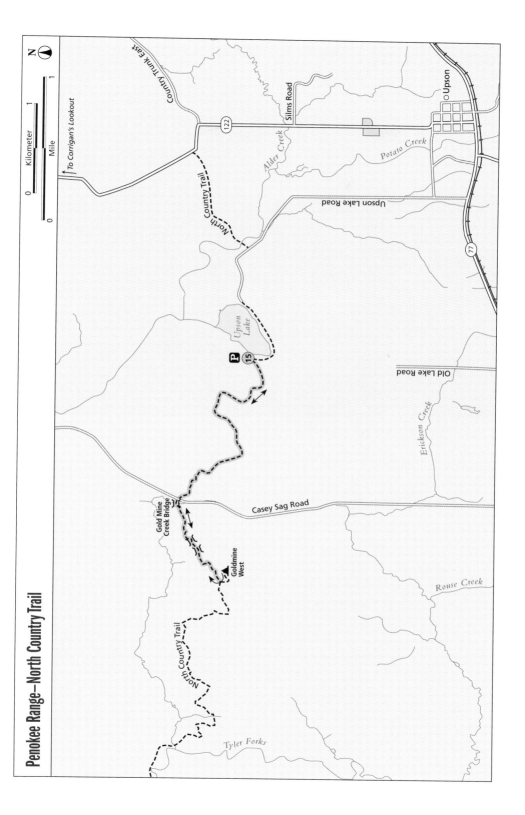

Elevated view of Upson Lake. DENICE BREAUX

high ridge, crossing a pair of short bridges en route. Just before a third bridge, a spur trail heads south to the Gold Mine West campsite, highly recommended for solitudi-nous splendor. Stay the night or turn back here to complete the route.

Miles and Directions

0.0 From the trailhead at the west end of Upson Lake, head west on the NCT, climbing a short ridge about 0.25 mile in.

2.7 At the junction with Casey Sag Road, cross the road and keep on truckin'.

3.1 Arrive at the Gold Mine West campsite. This is the turnaround point.

6.2 Arrive back at the trailhead.

Route alteration: You'll miss the Upson Lake view, but try starting at Casey Sag Road and hiking over the bridges and through some quintessential Penokee Range terrain to the road access near the Wren Falls campsite. It's about 3.5 miles one-way.

16 Madeline Island—Big Bay State Park

Half the fun is getting there with this pair of hikes on the largest and most southern of Lake Superior's Apostle Islands. Hop the Madeline Island Ferry and hit up Big Bay State Park for fairy-tale lake views and the best swimming beach on the South Shore, or go remote at the island's wilderness preserve.

Lake or river: Lake Superior and Big Bay
Photogenic factor: 5
Distance: 3.2-mile loop on the point; optional 2.0 miles out and back on the beach boardwalk
Difficulty: Easy to moderate
Hiking time: About 90 minutes for bay loop; 45 minutes to an hour for beach boardwalk
Trail surface: Hard-packed dirt and boardwalk

Other trail users: None
Canine compatibility: Leashed pets allowed on trails but not allowed on boardwalk
Land status: State park
Fees and permits: Vehicle pass required
Maps: State park maps; USGS Ashland
Trail contacts: Big Bay State Park, 2402 Hagen Rd., La Pointe 54850; (715) 747-6425; dnr.wi.gov/topic/parks/name/bigbay

Finding the trailhead: From Bayfield, board a Madeline Island Ferry or other vessel to reach the island. Once on the island in La Pointe, follow CR H east 3.8 miles to its junction with Hagen Road. Continue east on Hagen Road 2 miles to the park entrance. Find the trailhead at the day-use picnic areas. **Trailhead GPS:** N46 79.734' / W90 66.899'

The Hike

Throughout this book I write of the otherworldly power of glaciers and their impact on the Wisconsin we see today. Indeed, all corners of the state were created by the scouring of mile-high ice four times over, but what about the Apostle Islands?

HERMIT ISLAND

A couple of miles northwest of the northern tip of Madeline Island lies Hermit Island, a small oval of dense woods and low cliffs that hosted brownstone quarries from the early 1860s to 1890s. But the island is known more for its ghost than rocks. William Wilson, a resident of La Pointe on Madeline Island, lost a fistfight bet with the town's magistrate and was exiled to a nearby island. Wilson didn't mind it out there at all and made a decent living crafting barrels for the big lake ships. In the depths of the winter of 1861, no smoke had been seen from Wilson's island home for a few days and a posse discovered him dead inside the house. Murder was suspected and some say Wilson didn't take kindly to that, and his ghost still wanders the island today.

A lone sailboat on Big Bay. DENICE BREAUX

We don't often relate glaciers to islands, but the Apostles are actually 600-million-year-old remnants of enormous rocks left behind by glaciers in the Lake Superior basin. And these rocks are tough, hanging in there through 100,000 years of determined glacial events. Madeline Island emerged from the fray about 15,000 years ago, only to continue its metamorphosis at the hands of waves and currents, some of which constructed today's sandy beach and lagoon at Big Bay State Park.

It's only fitting that the largest of the Apostle Islands hosts a big ol' state park to match. Big Bay State Park is 2,300 acres of amazingness, with a riveting mix of ecosystems from the sandy shore to bogs to forested ridgeline. Adjacent to the park's campground is the wonderfully unique Big Bay Sand Spit and Bog, 440 acres of floating sphagnum-sedge bog, stately second-growth boreal forest, and a vibrant population of bog flora.

On a hot summer day, Big Bay's long, sprawling beach is the place to be, with plenty o' room to stretch out on a lounge chair, build a sandcastle, or paddle a kayak around the bay. The optional Boardwalk Trail is another don't-miss park highlight. The half-mile, flat trail parallels the beach on its way through an enchanting stand of red and white pines near the spit.

If you can pry yourself away from the already beauteous distractions near the bay, head for the Woods Trail for a view-packed hike along the rounded, woodsy nub above Lake Superior.

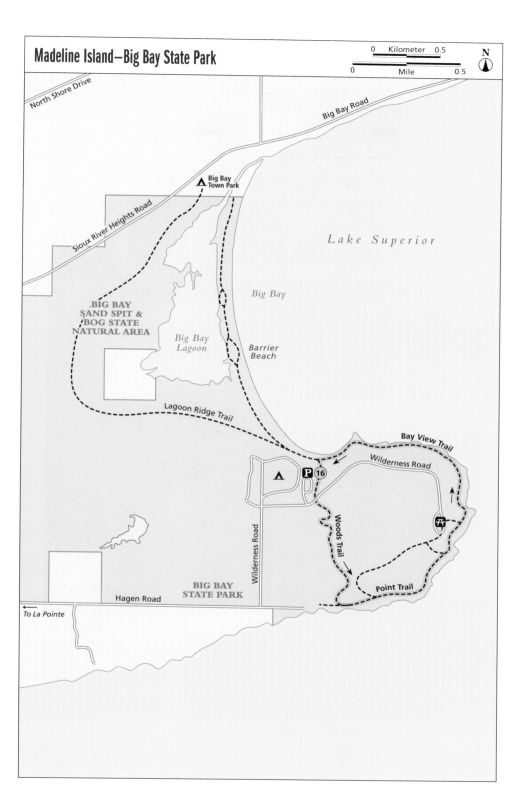

Madeline Island–Big Bay State Park

Kilometer 0 0.5

Mile 0 0.5

N

North Shore Drive

Big Bay Road

Big Bay Town Park

Sioux River Heights Road

Lake Superior

Big Bay

BIG BAY SAND SPIT & BOG STATE NATURAL AREA

Big Bay Lagoon

Barrier Beach

Lagoon Ridge Trail

Bay View Trail

Wilderness Road

P 16

Woods Trail

Wilderness Road

Point Trail

BIG BAY STATE PARK

Hagen Road

To La Pointe

Magnificent Lake Superior shoreline. DENICE BREAUX

Idyllic rest stop along the trail. DENICE BREAUX

Starting from the campground area, follow Woods Trail toward the southern end of the point and hop onto Point Trail. From here the path encounters a few mild ups and downs in terrain as it curves along the point. You will soon merge with Bay View Trail and be treated to several overlooks with beauteous views out over Lake Superior. A barely noticeable descent takes you back to the trailhead, where there's easy access to the don't-miss beach boardwalk trail.

Option: The boardwalk trail is a pan-flat treat tracking arrow-straight through an aged forest of pine, aspen, birch, and maple. The beach is only steps away if you feel a spontaneous urge to jump in, and the path also leads directly to the above-mentioned Big Bay Sand Spit. Good times, indeed.

Miles and Directions

0.0   From the trailhead, follow Woods Trail roughly southeast to the lakeshore and turn left on Point Trail.

1.2   Point Trail merges with Bay View Trail. Keep on hiking around the point. The path will lead right back to the trailhead.

3.2   Arrive back at the trailhead.

17 Madeline Island Wilderness Preserve

Come wander in one of Wisconsin's largest and blissfully primitive wilderness preserves, with 2,600 acres of elegant second-growth forest and big views of the big lake.

Lake or river: Lake Superior
Photogenic factor: 4
Distance: 4.8-mile loop or shorter out-and-
back options of your choosing
Difficulty: Easy
Hiking time: 2+ hours
Trail surface: Packed dirt and grass, with
intermittent wet sections

Other trail users: None
Canine compatibility: Leashed pets allowed
Land status: Nonprofit preserve
Fees and permits: None
Maps: Preserve maps; USGS Ashland
Trail contacts: Madeline Island Wilderness
Preserve, PO Box 28, La Pointe 54850; miwp
.org

Finding the trailhead: From La Pointe, follow Airport Road 3.5 miles northeast to its junction with North Shore Drive. Head north on North Shore Drive 6 miles to the trailhead on the left.
Trailhead GPS: N46 85.525' / W90 63.251'

The Hike

In a far too familiar refrain, Madeline Island's northern reaches came under pressure
to subdivide and sprout more homes. Concerned and farsighted residents gathered to
discuss the threat, pooled their energy and resources, and in 1987 formed the Madeline Island Wilderness Preserve to protect the island's fascinating natural areas.

MIWP is one of Wisconsin's oldest and most accomplished nonprofit land trusts,
managing 2,600 acres of resplendent northern hardwood forest of maple, birch, red
oak, aspen, and pockets of hemlock. The organization's efforts have made a tremen-
dous difference in preserving the island's interior lands, and conservation work continues today. We can all share great gratitude for their work as we venture out to
explore the area's hiking trails.

Birch log art along the trail. DENICE BREAUX

The preserve's wonderfully primitive trails wander through sometimes-
wet terrain, bog sections, and the
mosquitoes will love you in the summer. Long pants, sturdy hiking boots,
and bug repellent are highly recommended. Keep an eye on trail blazes
and don't rely on your cell phone as
service is sketchy at best out here.

This versatile loop looks like the
head and bust of a woodpecker, with

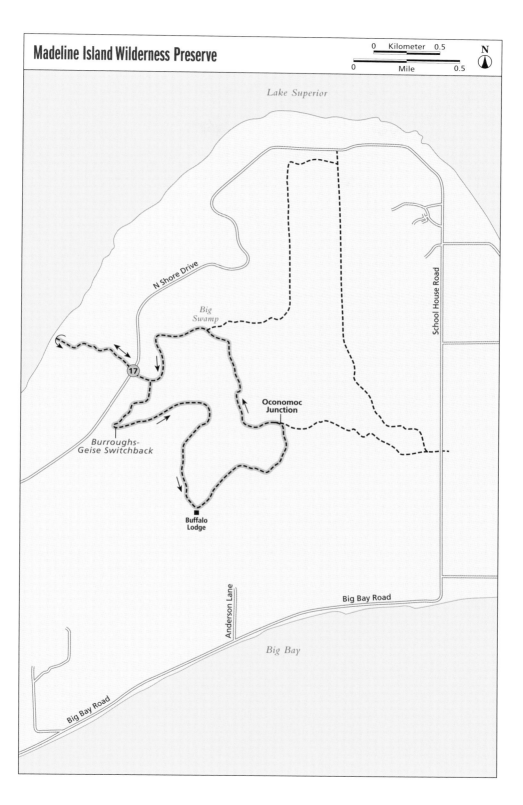

Madeline Island Wilderness Preserve

0 Kilometer 0.5
0 Mile 0.5

N

Lake Superior

N Shore Drive

Big Swamp

School House Road

17

Oconomoc Junction

Burroughs-Geise Switchback

Buffalo Lodge

Anderson Lane

Big Bay Road

Big Bay

Big Bay Road

a bonus trail thrown in. Start at the Burroughs Trailhead and hike northwesterly through the dense woods a little over a half mile to the shoreline for killer views of Lake Superior. Head back to the trailhead, cross the road, and turn right at the junction. This direction takes you on a gently sloping course through way-out-there forest of maple, birch, poplar, oak, and scattered stands of cedar and a hemlock or three.

Pass the Burroughs-Geise switchback and curve south past the Buffalo Lodge site and up to Oconomoc Junction. Go left here on a northwesterly track to Big Swamp and the final return to the trailhead. The entire loop pushes 5 miles, but you can shorten it by doing an out-and-back hike of whatever distance and direction you like.

Another wonderful highlight of the preserve is covered in black fur. We rarely see them on Madeline or the other Apostle Islands, but the National Park Service notes that neighboring Stockton Island alone saw an increase from just two bears in 1984 to thirty-one in 1994. Their numbers have fallen since then but the great beasts still roam the woods. Remember, fellow hiker, to keep your distance if you do encounter a bear, make a lot of racket, and try to make yourself look bigger. Personally, I'm not exactly convinced anything I do would scare off a 600-pound male, but it would be great to see one eating from a blackberry bush way over there or from the inside of a shark cage or something.

Miles and Directions

0.0 From the trailhead, hike west toward the lake, soak in the view, and return to start the loop. Turn right at the junction across the road and hike southwest.

3.4 At Oconomoc Junction, turn left.

4.2 Turn left at the Big Swamp junction.

4.8 Arrive back at the trailhead.

18 North Lakeland Discovery Trails

From young kids learning about butterflies to esteemed scientists conducting critical research, the Discovery Center is a wonderful place of learning and giving back, with relaxing and engaging hiking trails to connect with it all.

Lake or river: Statehouse Lake
Photogenic factor: 4
Distance: 1.2-mile loop
Difficulty: Easy
Hiking time: About 45 minutes
Trail surface: Hard-packed dirt path and some boardwalk
Other trail users: None

Canine compatibility: Leashed pets allowed
Land status: Private
Fees and permits: None
Maps: Discovery center maps; USGS Winchester
Trail contacts: North Lakeland Discovery Center, 14006 Discovery Ln., Manitowish Waters 54545; (877) 543-2085; discoverycenter.net

Finding the trailhead: From the village of Manitowish Waters at US 51, follow CR W north 1.2 miles to Discovery Lane and turn left. Follow this road 0.3 mile to the center. The trails begin adjacent to the center's main building. **Trailhead GPS:** N46 14.797' / W89 89.427'

The Hike

The North Lakeland Discovery Center is the mother lode of nature-based activity, from children's outings to scientific research, all of which showcases and works to preserve this enchanting area of Wisconsin.

Young and old, casual and formal, the education center hosts the likes of youth nature groups, state wildlife and ecosystem organizations, birding and gardening clubs, and an active citizen science group taking part in Monarch tagging, wolf howl surveys, crane counts, and Christmas bird counts.

The center is a nature-based education and community gathering place encouraging responsible and enriching use of Wisconsin's Northland. Part of their mission

NORTHWOODS BIRDING FESTIVAL

The Discovery Center hosts a very popular birding festival every year at the center and various locations around northern Wisconsin. Held at the end of May, the event brings in esteemed speakers, authors, environmental professionals, and other notables, and field trips take place throughout. Participants enjoy hiking outings to places like the Van Vliet Hemlocks, Frog Lake, and Presque Isle; photography tours; and, of course, all kinds of birding trips. Free guided nature hikes happen regularly, along with teen retreats, investigative canoe trips, invasive species–identification training, and cycling days with a naturalist.

Peaceful and calm Statehouse Lake. DENICE BREAUX

statement rings especially true: "Enriching lives and inspiring an ethic of care for Wisconsin's Northwoods."

Nice. Among the center's programs are nature study and recreation opportunities for groups such as the Center for Conservation Leadership and the Wisconsin Land+Water Youth Conservation Camp. Groups like these are treated to an incomparable teaching and learning environment packed with lakes, forests, and bogs. The center also hosts wildly popular birding events and outings, naturalist programs, a garden club, and intensive invasive-species research and removal efforts.

The Nature Nook is a cozy destination for children of all ages that houses a stocked nature-education library, youth activities, and a rotating lineup of area critters. All manner of year-round recreation opportunities tops it off. No doubt about it, this place is chock-full of outdoor goodness.

Yep, the pride of and dedication for nature is palpable here at the center and all along the hiking trails. Like this short and vibrant loop around Statehouse Lake, with a section of boardwalk through a bog and wildlife all over the place. From the trailhead, hike along the west side of the interpretive trail, paralleling the bog on your left. The boardwalk section starts at the top of the loop and is a glorious walk through a fascinating world of spongy, mossy ground; miniature ecosystems; and parades of birch and aspen and little white pines. I'm a huge fan of bogs and relish any opportunity to walk through one and find myself stopping every 10 feet to look and listen.

About halfway around the loop, the trail meets the junction with the Lookout Trail, which also connects to the Little Bit Longer Loop (love that name), Statehouse,

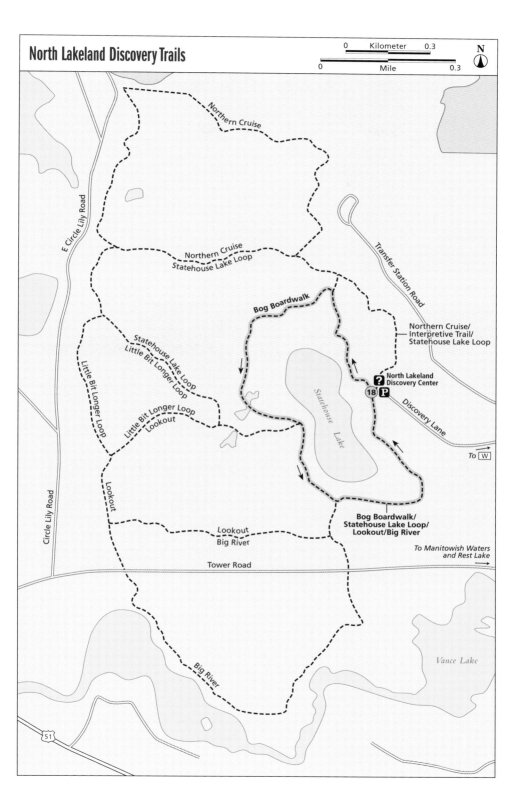

North Lakeland Discovery Trails

0   Kilometer   0.3
0   Mile   0.3

N

Northern Cruise

E Circle Lily Road

Transfer Station Road

Northern Cruise
Statehouse Lake Loop

Bog Boardwalk

Northern Cruise/
Interpretive Trail/
Statehouse Lake Loop

Statehouse Lake Loop
Little Bit Longer Loop

Little Bit Longer Loop

North Lakeland
Discovery Center

18

Little Bit Longer Loop
Lookout

Statehouse
Lake

Lookout

Discovery Lane

To W

Circle Lily Road

Lookout
Big River

Bog Boardwalk/
Statehouse Lake Loop/
Lookout/Big River

To Manitowish Waters
and Rest Lake

Tower Road

Vance Lake

Big River

51

Well-marked trails lead the way. DENICE BREAUX

The Nature Nook. DENICE BREAUX

and Big River Trails. Score great views of Statehouse Lake from here and then angle southeast and around the south end of the lake to the homestretch to the trailhead.

Miles and Directions

0.0 Hike north from the trailhead on the Bog Boardwalk Trail.

0.1 Junction with the start of the boardwalk.

0.5 At the trail junction with outer trails, keep heading south.

1.2 Arrive back at the trailhead.

19 Van Vliet Hemlocks State Natural Area

One-tenth of 1 percent is all that remains of Wisconsin's original old-growth forests. The Van Vliet stand offers a rare opportunity to walk among these noble trees.

Lake or river: Van Vliet and Hemlock Lakes
Photogenic factor: 5
Distance: 3.2-mile loop for perimeter trail; shorter loop options available
Difficulty: Easy
Hiking time: About 90 minutes
Trail surface: Hard-packed dirt path
Other trail users: None

Canine compatibility: Leashed pets allowed
Land status: State of Wisconsin
Fees and permits: None
Maps: DNR maps; USGS Wakefield, MI
Trail contacts: Wisconsin Department of Natural Resources, 101 S. Webster St., Madison 53707; (888) 936-7463; dnr.wi.gov/topic/Lands/naturalareas/index.asp?SNA=673

Finding the trailhead: From CR B and Crab Lake Road in Presque Isle, head south on Crab Lake Road for 3.7 miles to East Van Vliet Road. Turn right and follow Van Vliet Road 0.9 mile to the trailhead. **Trailhead GPS:** N46 19.840' / W89 75.060'

The Hike

Hemlocks once reigned in northern Wisconsin's forests, but in the latter half of the 1800s, hemlocks and virtually all the rest of the state's timber was cut or burned and old-growth here today is nearly nonexistent.

The Van Vliet Hemlocks are a rare vestige of these regal trees and this is one of the state's largest stands of its kind. In fact, hikers today are treated to a genuine old-growth forest vibe—fallen giants cloaked in emerald-green moss, glacial moraines, bogs, wetlands, vernal pools, and lakes. The woods today are dominated by eastern hemlock, sugar maple, and paper and yellow birch, with patches of basswood, red oak, and white pine. The shrub layer is sparse aside from thickets of elderberry, honeysuckle, and the like.

This forest is a critical link in protecting ecologically vibrant and undeveloped lake frontage. That all blends together to make a stunningly beautiful forest and we are fortunate to share its space.

Bald eagles and loons are common here, nesting annually, as are scarlet tanagers, warblers including the blackburnian and black-throated green varieties, pileated woodpeckers, hermit thrush, nuthatch, and myriad other songbirds and waterfowl. Understory flora species are equally vibrant. Look for lily of the valley, jack-in-the-pulpit, and lots of maidenhair fern.

Also of note from a geologic perspective is a subcontinental divide at about 1,700 feet. This moraine sends water north of it to Lake Superior and water on the other side flows south to the Mississippi River. Cheers to the glaciers for creating topography like this, as well as cedar swamps, bog lakes, and steep esker ridgelines.

HIDDEN HEMLOCK TREASURE

Did you know that hemlock trees fueled a booming leather industry in the late 1800s? Tannins found in the bark of hemlocks were essential ingredients in the leather-tanning process. Millions of trees were felled and stripped of their bark, which was hauled to tanneries in cities like Milwaukee. In the early 1900s, Wisconsin was the nation's leading supplier of "tanning bark." All the trees were gone, but at least you could have a wallet in your pocket.

Start this short hike by following a section of Van Vliet Lake shoreline. In a short while you'll meet up with the Yellow Birch Loop. Keep on the western edge of this trail to the Bog Loop. Go west again to circle around the bog. From there, the route traces the southern edge of the Hemlock Lake Loop for a chance to see these resplendent trees before reaching the homestretch section to the trailhead.

On your hike, remember that this place is a rare treat in large part due to the Friends of the Van Vliet Hemlocks, an affiliate group of the North Lakeland Discovery Center. This dedicated group leads nature walks and pitches in with trail projects and related work in the area, all in the name of preserving the irreplaceable natural beauty around us.

A calm day on the lake. DENICE BREAUX

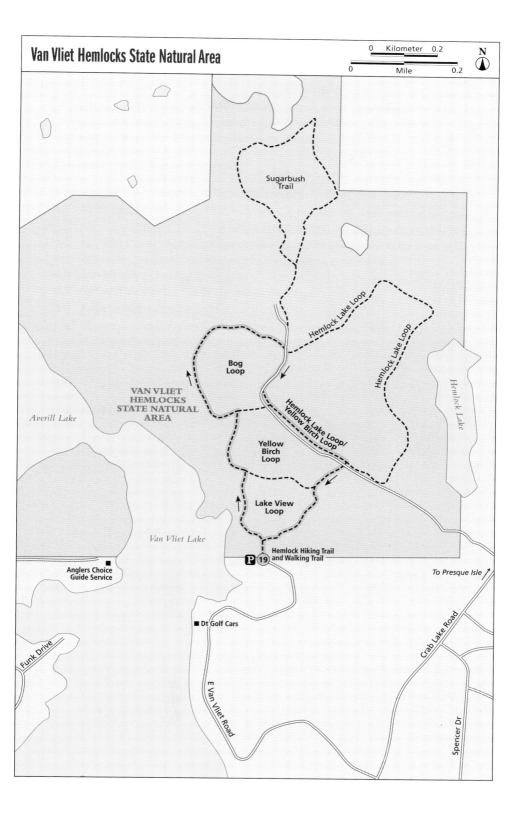

Van Vliet Hemlocks State Natural Area

Sugarbush
Trail

Hemlock Lake Loop

Hemlock Lake Loop

Hemlock Lake Loop

Hemlock Lake

Bog
Loop

VAN VLIET
HEMLOCKS
STATE NATURAL
AREA

Averill Lake

Hemlock Lake Loop/
Yellow Birch Loop

Yellow
Birch
Loop

Lake View
Loop

Van Vliet Lake

Hemlock Hiking Trail
and Walking Trail

P 19

Anglers Choice
Guide Service

To Presque Isle

Dt Golf Cars

Funk Drive

E Van Vliet Road

Crab Lake Road

Spencer Dr

N

0   Kilometer   0.2

0   Mile   0.2

Scenic forest on the Lake View Loop. DENICE BREAUX

Miles and Directions

0.0 From the trailhead, go left and hike along the west side of the Lake View Loop.

0.2 Turn left here to follow the Yellow Birch Loop.

0.4 Turn left again on the Bog Loop Trail.

0.9 At the junction with Sugarbush and Hemlock Lake Trails, turn right. Follow the combined trails southeast, looping back along Yellow Birch and Lake View to reach the trailhead.

3.2 Arrive back at the trailhead.

20 Fallison Lake Trail

A Wisconsin hiking book is not complete without the outrageously beautiful Fallison Lake Trail. With four loop options, old-growth splendor, and a Northwoods-perfect lake, this author favorite is a don't-miss destination for unforgettable trail miles.

Lake or river: Fallison Lake
Photogenic factor: 5
Distance: 2.0-mile loop; 1.0- and 5.0-mile loops also available
Difficulty: Moderate for long loop; rolling hills throughout
Hiking time: About 90 minutes
Trail surface: Hard-packed dirt path and boardwalk

Other trail users: None
Canine compatibility: Pets not allowed
Land status: State of Wisconsin
Fees and permits: None
Maps: DNR maps; USGS Rhinelander
Trail contacts: Wisconsin Department of Natural Resources, 101 S. Webster St., Madison 53707; (888) 936-7463; dnr.wi.gov/topic/Lands/naturalareas/index.asp?

Finding the trailhead: From Boulder Junction, follow CR M south approximately 9 miles to CR N. Turn east on CR N and go 2.3 miles to the trailhead across from Crystal Lake Campground.
Trailhead GPS: N45 99.812' / W89 61.756'

The Hike

An elegantly beautiful forest of white pine, maple, birch, balsam, and aspen; a hemlock glade; bogs and boardwalks, all surrounding a clear northern lake. Even better, this is one of those hidden gems in an already opulent gallery.

The Fallison Lake area is nothing short of phenomenal. Scenic sights are packed into every step of this hike and the path is clearly signed along the way. Several benches offer perfect perches to soak in views of the lake, and interpretive signs show all kinds of fascinating beta about local critters, flora, and geologic wonders. Picnic tables and a water pump are conveniently located among some rare hemlocks roughly at the loop's halfway point, and a bonus trail loops around an open bog east of the lake.

Start this hike on a counterclockwise track through resplendent forest heavy in hardwood species, with a conifer or three thrown in for good measure. You'll walk through sugar maple, aspen, white birch, and scatterings of balsam, red, and white pine. The path follows the outline of the lake but stays a bit inland to start, following undulating terrain with intermittent sections of steps and a short boardwalk. Along the way, a few wooden benches offer excellent rest stops and reflection time nearer the water. At the south end of the loop, a water pump waits like a mirage in the desert—gloriously cold and delicious at the perfect time.

From here the path curves back north but not without first passing one of the most peaceful and postcard-perfect settings I've seen up here. It's a treat to be part

A tranquil bay on Fallison Lake.

Postcard view of Fallison Lake.

of the picture and a wonderful place to linger awhile with views north of nearly the entire 50-acre lake and a great opportunity to spot resident loons, bald eagles, and osprey. Behind you is a tamarack bog so vivid with color and scent and aura, it seems painted there by a skilled hand. Be on the lookout for beaver activity hereabouts.

Follow the path up a long set of steps into conifer-heavy forest; quite a contrast from the lake's more hardwood-filled western side. A handful of benches offers more incredible views and quiet time. (Some of the views are obscured in summer, but return in fall for a look at the lake through fiery golden leaves.) A little more than

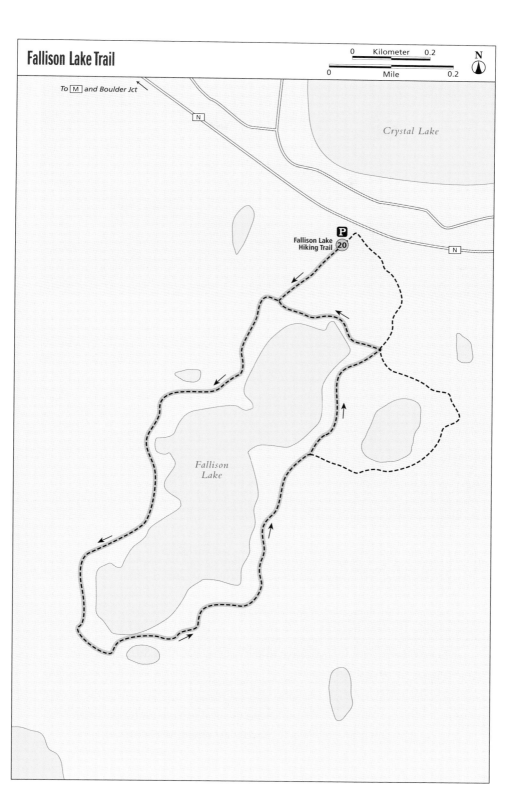

Fallison Lake Trail

To M and Boulder Jct

N

Crystal Lake

P
Fallison Lake
Hiking Trail 20

N

Fallison
Lake

Natural trail art.

halfway back up the shoreline, you'll meet the junction with the short loop around a little bog lake, another tailor-made destination for channeling your inner nature child. Continue north along the lake to another junction.

From the junction, turn left here and you'll hike through several more gentle swales before arriving back at the trailhead. ***Bonus trail tip:*** This loop is perfect for snowshoeing so be sure to come back when the snow flies.

Miles and Directions

0.0 From the trailhead, follow the path south from the kiosk.

0.1 Go right at this junction to start the loop.

0.9 Arrive at the south end of the lake. Refill your water bottle at the pump and linger with the lake views.

1.6 At the junction with the trail around the bog lake, continue straight ahead.

1.8 Go left at this junction, hiking past the north end of the lake.

2.0 Arrive back at the trailhead.

THE SONG OF THE VIREO

You're in for a treat if the red-eyed vireo is in a singing mood out here. When not eating insects, larvae, or berries, the vireo sings and really gets into it. You have to hear it to fully appreciate the melody, but in human-speak the vireo song is a series of simple three-verse phrases whistled in a hurry. Each verse often closes with a downward note or an uptick, like the asking and answering of a question. It's best to just sit still and listen.

21 Star Lake Trail and Plum Lake Hemlock Forest SNA

This is the author's pick for the best hike in the state. A bold statement backed up by ridiculously beautiful scenery, heavenly trails, and conservation-based history.

Lake or river: Star Lake
Photogenic factor: 4
Distance: 2.5-mile loop
Difficulty: Easy to moderate
Hiking time: About 90 minutes
Trail surface: Hard-packed dirt path
Other trail users: None
Canine compatibility: Pets not allowed on Star Lake Trail; leashed pets allowed in Plum Lake SNA

Land status: State of Wisconsin
Fees and permits: None
Maps: DNR maps; USGS Wakefield, MI
Trail contacts: Wisconsin Department of Natural Resources, 101 S. Webster St., Madison 53707; (888) 936-7463; dnr.wi.gov/topic/Lands/naturalareas/index.asp

Finding the trailhead: From the town of Sayner, follow CR N 5.6 miles north to CR K and turn left. Follow CR K 0.5 mile west to Statehouse Road and turn left. In 0.4 mile this road ends at the trailhead. **Trailhead GPS:** N46 03.266' / W89 47.746'

The Hike

I'm just going to come right out and say it: This is my favorite hiking trail in the state. I relished every single step and more than one time had to pry myself away from one idyllic place only to be captivated by another. I'm no world traveler but I've been fortunate to hike all over the country, from ocean-side getaways to the rarified air of mountaintops, and for all-around "unforgettableness," this short little hike in northern Wisconsin is tops on the list.

Steeped in history and otherworldly scenery, this trail is made of ideal hiking tread, with a layer of pine needles and sandy soil creating a spongy feel that puts a natural spring in your step. Gnarled and determined roots furrow the trail, and boulders of various sizes punctuate the path in all the right places. Fittingly, the Star Lake Trail is located on a narrow peninsula jutting into its namesake lake, and to the joy of hikers everywhere, the trail traces the squiggly shoreline all the way around.

In some places the path takes you close enough to dip your toes in the lake (or jump right in). Other sections are elevated for stop-in-your-tracks views, especially on the eastern side, with beeline views of a pair of islands way across the lake. At the southern tip of the peninsula is a place that inspires all manner of nature-based daydreams: Elegant, soaring white pines shade a picnic-perfect scene, with a fire pit

The trail to the pines.   *The trail in all its splendor.*

and water's-edge views of the lake. There's even a little beach here for spontaneous swims. Heavenly.

From here the path shows off just enough up and down to make it interesting, and one of my favorite sights is a huge, shoreside cedar that tied itself into a knot as it grew around a boulder. A fascinating display of resolve, and I bet you can't untie that knot!

This is a great path for all ages and abilities, made even better with its deep historical roots. Did you know that this peninsula hosted Wisconsin's first tree nursery, inspired by our first state forester? E. M. Griffith believed in replanting the Northland after the ravages of logging, and under his guidance, a red pine plantation plot was planted here in 1913 with seedlings grown at the old Trout Lake Nursery in Boulder Junction. Griffith planted native red and white pine, along with Scotch pine for its rapid growth rate. Today you can see vivid evidence of the plantation experiment and walk among the giant trees.

Hike this loop clockwise by hiking west from the trailhead, down a gradual slope to a quick left, following the nature trail sign. Keep heading southwest and cross a scenic boardwalk section, then emerge to 180-degree views of the lake. From here the path traces the shoreline on a super-fun, gently undulating track to the southern end of the peninsula. Here is where you'll find that cover-shot picnic spot and you can't go any farther without stopping to savor this place—those are the rules.

Star Lake Trail and Plum Lake Hemlock Forest SNA

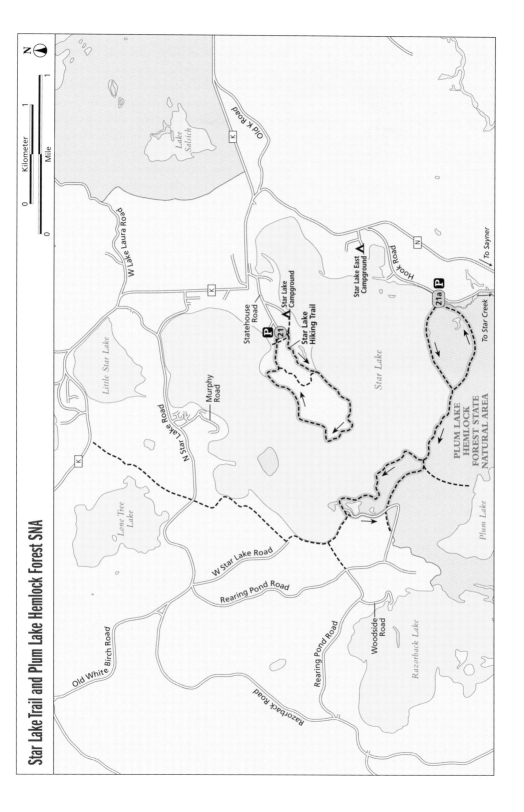

White pines frame Star Lake.

Roll on from here up along the western shore, with more beauteous views that will make you stumble over your own feet. After the trail turns inland, it meets one more junction where you'll turn left and wander through another stand of regal pines on the way back to the trailhead.

As a close to this chapter, I'd like you to think about the 1800s logging mania. In a sixteen-year blink of time, original old-growth forest hundreds of years old was razed. The people came, took what they wanted, and left behind nothing but stumps and rubble. Today, far more people are of the same mind-set, and for lack of better words, we are beating our planet into submission. I hope more of us will channel our inner E. M. Griffith, or Leopold, or Muir, and work to save more special places like this.

Miles and Directions

0.0 From the trailhead, hike due west on the main path.

0.2 Turn left here toward the lake.

1.6 Take the right fork here and pass through a bog area.

2.1 Take a left turn back to the trailhead.

2.5 Arrive back at the trailhead.

THERE AND GONE

Following a very familiar refrain in the logging era, the bustling town of Star Lake emerged virtually overnight in the late 1800s, with around 600 hardy souls hustling about a menagerie of warehouses, offices, a hotel, a school, and a railroad depot. And it was all about trees. An estimated *2 billion* board feet of pine timber was logged clear from lands around Star Lake. When the trees were gone, the town disappeared as well.

21a Trampers Trails

See map on page 87.
Lake or river: Star Lake
Photogenic factor: 4+
Distance: 4.1-mile loop

Difficulty: Moderate
Hiking time: About 2 hours
Trail surface: Hard-packed dirt

Finding the trailhead: From the village of Star Lake at the junction of CR K and CR N, follow CR N south 0.9 mile to a skinny forest road just past the Star Lake East campground. Look for the little Trampers Trails sign. Follow that road 1 mile south to its end at the trailhead. **Trailhead GPS:** N46 01.293' / W89 47.185'

The Hike

This trail gets my vote for the best off-the-grid, way-out-there remote path. Tucked partly in the Plum Lake Hemlock Forest SNA, this route is part of a wonderfully squiggly maze of a trail system that wanders the woods all the way around the south and west side of Star Lake and back to CR N.

The path mixes it up with taking you get-your-feet-wet close to the water, rugged sections of roots and rocks on punchy little hills, and stretches of calm in the trees. This is yet another of my all-time favorite trails, in large part due to its remote vibe, old-growth forest lineage, and silent invitation to just go out there and do what it's named for: tramping!

With every step of this hike, know that you are traveling through a near-virgin stand of old-growth forest packed with the likes of über-rare hemlock, yellow and paper birch, sugar maple, and basswood. Forestry experts tell us that the presence of large, aged white birch means this stand likely was born of a fire event around 1810 with a natural succession of species from aspen to hemlock. Shrub species in attendance include mountain maple, honeysuckle, and elderberry; and below you will see mayflower, plentiful emerald-green moss, snowberry, and lots more. Flitting about this paradise are dozens of songbird species, merrily singing away the praises of calling this place home.

We can join in their song, simultaneously content and proud to be in such good company and treasured legacy. SNAs like this one are Wisconsin's last refuges for rare plant and animal species. More than 90 percent of plants and 75 percent of endangered and threatened species in our state are protected within SNAs. Many of these places provide critical living laboratories for scientific research due to their visible evidence of natural processes evolving with very little human muddling. And that is the most priceless of heirlooms to share with generations to come.

The entire first half of the loop traces very close to Star Lake's shoreline with the expected gorgeous views, and the trail is a blast; full of personality in the form

Island view from Plum Lake Hemlock SNA.

of scattered boulders of various girth and of course the resplendent hemlock forest. At the top side of the western loop, the trail skirts around a little pond and it is here where, if you're ambitious, you can keep right on hiking for the rest of the day.

This time, however, head back south and link up with the connector trail along the shore back to the first loop, and follow the south leg back to the trailhead.

Miles and Directions

0.0 Follow the trail along the lake.

0.7 At the first junction, go straight ahead.

1.2 Take the right fork here, following the shoreline.

2.1 At the junction at the top side of this loop, head straight, going south.

2.4 Veer left at this junction.

2.8 Turn left here and make a quick right back along the shore trail.

3.3 At the junction with the first loop, go right and complete the circle back to the trailhead.

4.1 Arrive back at the trailhead.

LAKES!

Vilas County is home to upwards of 1,320 lakes, one of the highest densities of lakes on Earth. Roughly 900 of these are here in the Northern Highland-American Legion State Forest.

22 Franklin Lake Trail

This short, scenic loop is jam-packed with unforgettable highlights like a long board-walk, tamarack bog, and human history dating to *8000 BC*.

Lake or river: Franklin and Butternut Lakes
Photogenic factor: 5
Distance: 1.0-mile loop
Difficulty: Easy
Hiking time: 45–60 minutes
Trail surface: Gravel and hard-packed dirt path with occasional roots or rocks
Other trail users: None
Canine compatibility: Leashed pets allowed

Land status: Chequamegon-Nicolet National Forest
Fees and permits: Vehicle pass required
Maps: National forest maps; USGS Rhinelander, WI; Iron Mountain, MI
Trail contacts: Chequamegon-Nicolet National Forest, 500 Hansen Rd., Rhinelander 54501; (715) 362-1300; fs.usda.gov/cnnf

Finding the trailhead: From the intersection of WI 70 and US 45 at the eastern fringe of Eagle River, follow WI 70 east 7.6 miles to Military Road (FR 2178) and turn right. In 2.5 miles, turn left on Butternut Lake Road (FR 2181). Follow this road 4.4 miles to the nature trail parking area.
Trailhead GPS: N45 92.580' / W88 99.586'

The Hike

Twenty-one numbered interpretive stations dot the length of the Franklin Nature Trail, calling out the array of enchanting Northwoods wonders. The trail is mostly flat, with a few easygoing undulations here and there as it lopes through a dense forest of soaring white pine, noble hemlocks, and mixed hardwoods like maple, birch, ash, and aspen.

One of my favorite parts of the hike is the 400 feet of boardwalk through a tamarack bog filled with puffy sphagnum moss veiled in spruce and tamarack stands, and the shorter one leading to amazing views of Butternut Lake. Low-to-the-ground plant life thrives in the bog in the form of leatherleaf, bog laurel and rosemary, pitcher plant, and wild blueberries. The adjoining woods are home to equally elegant plant species—look for bunchberry, starflower, jack-in-the-pulpit, and bluebead lily to name but a few.

This is a very popular camping and outdoor recreation destination and includes a collection of masterfully crafted, distinctive buildings and other structures built by the Civilian Conservation Corps and granting this place a spot on the National Register of Historic Places.

And that is part of the reason that this is another author favorite trail. It reminds me of Oregon, with huge, fallen logs cloaked in emerald-green moss, big, big trees more than 400 years old, and a boardwalk through an über-quiet tamarack bog. The

Franklin Lake on a windy summer day.

trail stays mostly flat until reaching the west side when it lopes up a short, punchy climb to the top of a glacial esker. I'm a big fan of eskers and would go as far to say they're my favorite glacial artwork. This one includes a bonus of a mysterious, old stone building within arm's reach of the trail.

Past the stone hut, the trail gradually descends back to the trailhead. There's a good chance that, like me, you'll feel like the hike ended too soon, but never fear—this is just a primer trail. There are lots of additional hiking miles out here, including the 15-mile Hidden Lakes Trail, Luna–White Deer Trail at 4 miles, and the Anvil Recreation Trail at 12 miles. Mountain-bike trails and untold miles of smooth, paved roads are also available for cycling. Franklin Lake's campground hosts nearly eighty

THE CIVILIAN CONSERVATION CORPS

One of President Franklin D. Roosevelt's initiatives was implementing programs to improve a Depression-beleaguered economy and people, and one huge success story is the Civilian Conservation Corps (CCC). Once enrolled in the CCC, young men worked on projects focused on environmental conservation and outdoor recreation promotion. In return, they received food, clothing, shelter, education, job training, and money for their families. They created landscapes, trails, roads, and campsites in national and state parks, incorporating rustic aesthetics into settings using logs, boulders, and other natural materials. Franklin Lake Campground is testament to this ethic, with the largest collection of rustic buildings, virtually unaltered since construction, in Wisconsin's national forest lands. All told, more than 75,000 Wisconsin men worked with the CCC.

Franklin Lake Trail

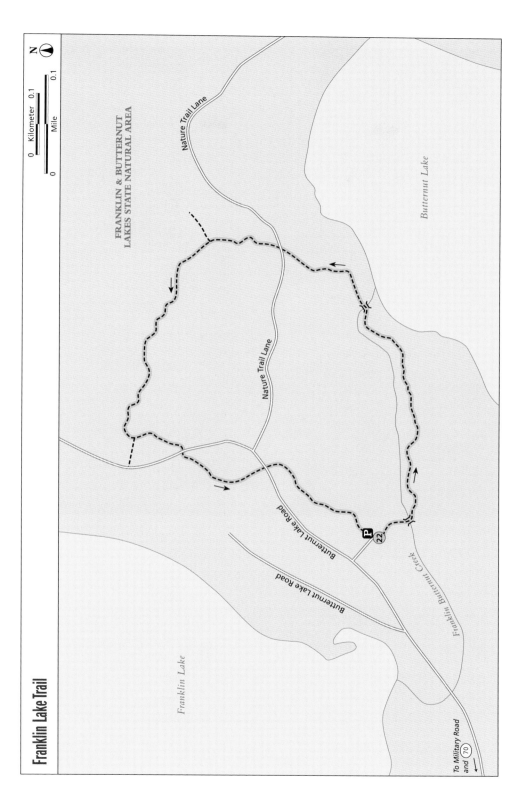

FRANKLIN & BUTTERNUT
LAKES STATE NATURAL AREA

Nature Trail Lane

Nature Trail Lane

Butternut Lake Road

Butternut Lake Road

Franklin Lake

Butternut Lake

Franklin Butternut Creek

To Military Road
and 70

N

0   Kilometer   0.1

0   Mile   0.1

P   22

Boardwalk view of Franklin Lake.

sites with great lake views and lots of shade and drinking water. Find seventy-one more campsites at the Luna-White Deer and Spectacle Lake locations. Plan on staying awhile!

Miles and Directions

0.0   From the trailhead, hike south across Butternut Creek and follow the squiggly trail south of the creek.

0.2   Turn right at the short boardwalk for sweet views of Butternut Lake.

0.3   Cross Nature Trail Lane.

0.5   Pass through the tamarack bog.

0.6   At Butternut Lake Road, angle southwest to cross it one more time.

1.0   Arrive back at the trailhead.

23 Catherine Wolter Wilderness Trails

The blissfully remote Catherine Wolter Wilderness is a 2,600-acre playground filled with fifteen lakes and wild critters and a healthy dose of solitude. Paradise found.

Lake or river: Knife and Canteen Lakes
Photogenic factor: 4
Distance: 2.8-mile main loop; optional 1.0-mile round-trip trail to Knife Lake
Difficulty: Moderate with several short and steep hills
Hiking time: About 90 minutes
Trail surface: Hard-packed dirt and mowed grass paths
Other trail users: None

Canine compatibility: Leashed pets allowed
Land status: State of Wisconsin; The Nature Conservancy
Fees and permits: None
Maps: The Nature Conservancy and Vilas County maps; USGS Wakefield, MI
Trail contacts: Wisconsin Department of Natural Resources, 101 S. Webster St., Madison 53707; (888) 936-7463; dnr.wi.gov/topic/Lands/naturalareas/index.asp?

Finding the trailhead: From Presque Isle, follow CR B southeast 3 miles to East Bay Road and turn left. Follow East Bay Road 0.6 mile to the trailhead on the right.
Trailhead GPS: N46 22.988' / W89 67.293'

The Hike

Staples in the Presque Isle area for sixty years, Fred and Catherine Wolter homesteaded a magnificent property near Wisconsin's northern border. After her husband passed, Catherine continued caring for the property until June of 2000 when The Nature Conservancy purchased the land as the first parcel for a wilderness preserve.

The wide path through dense woods. DENICE BREAUX

Lily pads on Knife Lake. DENICE BREAUX

In October of that year, University of Wisconsin–Milwaukee researchers launched an intensive study of the preserve's lakes and groundwater to assess water quality, and expanded the study to include a comprehensive inventory of plant and animal life in area lakes. Data from the study still influence land-management decisions.

Today the Catherine Wolter Wilderness Preserve and Border Lakes SNA includes more than 2,600 acres, fifteen wild lakes with thriving native fish populations (some of the last in Wisconsin lakes) and a host of waterfowl species, and forests chock-full of vibrant flora and fauna. Some of the critters living in or visiting the area are black bears, timber wolves, fishers, otters, and a spirited chorus of migrant songbirds.

Of special importance is 10 miles of undeveloped shoreline on lakes including Knife, Bug, Canteen, and Battine. Undeveloped shoreline is a rarity these days, and we can all toast the Wolters and dedicated Nature Conservancy efforts for making it happen.

The Musolf loop is nearly 3 miles around, with a 1-mile spur trail leading to Knife Lake. With the exception of a few level stretches, the trail undulates and throws in a handful of short, punchy hills for good measure. You'll walk start to finish through dense hardwood forest, starting with a gradual uphill track to the Knife Lake spur trail. The spur trail descends gently through a formerly logged stand of trees to the

CONSERVATION VISION

In 1945 Fred and Catherine Wolter moved from Milwaukee to the tiny town of Winegar in Wisconsin's far north. Like most folks in those days, the Wolters struggled, but Fred ran for and eventually won the town chairman seat, which he held for twelve years. Arguably his most significant accomplishment, the results of which we still appreciate today, was passing waterfront-development ordinances. All newly divided lakefront lots had to be at least 1.5 acres and include a minimum of 200 feet of lake frontage. This ordinance quickly set a standard throughout the state and is largely responsible for the peace and quiet we so fondly treasure in the Northland.

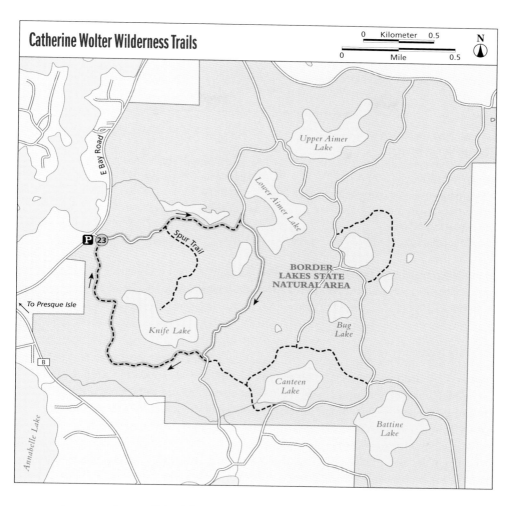

0   Kilometer   0.5

0   Mile   0.5

N

Upper Aimer Lake

Lower Aimer Lake

Spur Trail

P 23

E Bay Road

← To Presque Isle

BORDER LAKES STATE NATURAL AREA

Bug Lake

Knife Lake

B

Canteen Lake

Battine Lake

Annabelle Lake

northeastern shore of the lake, and when you get back to the main track, the path curves through a short stretch of dense pine/hardwood forest and along a spit of land between Lower Aimer Lake and another little tadpole-shaped lake. Drop through a shallow valley and then down toward the eastern end of Knife Lake.

A little bump in the path leads to the junction with the trail to Canteen Lake. Pass by this one and cruise a level section before reaching a gradual climb near the western nose of Knife Lake and the downhill run to the trailhead.

Miles and Directions

0.0   Hike east from the trailhead.

1.5   At the junction with the Canteen Lake trail, turn right. Follow this L-shaped stretch all the way back to the trailhead.

2.8   Arrive back at the trailhead.

24 Lauterman Lake Trail

Want to get off the grid? This wildly scenic hike on a lumpy, lakeside trail shares billing with some of Wisconsin's most remote campsites.

Lake or river: Lauterman Lake
Photogenic factor: 4+
Distance: 3.0-mile loop
Difficulty: Moderate
Hiking time: About 90 minutes
Trail surface: Hard-packed dirt path
Other trail users: None
Canine compatibility: Leashed pets allowed

Land status: Chequamegon-Nicolet National Forest
Fees and permits: Daily parking fee required
Maps: National forest maps; USGS Iron Mountain, MI
Trail contacts: Chequamegon-Nicolet National Forest, 500 Hansen Rd., Rhinelander 54501; (715) 362-1300; fs.usda.gov/cnnf

Finding the trailhead: From the town of Florence, follow WI 70 12.4 miles west to FR 2154 and turn left. The trailhead is 0.1 mile farther on the left. **Trailhead GPS:** N45 92.326' / W88 49.771'

The Hike

Backpackers and tent campers rejoice! In Wisconsin's far northeastern corner, close to the state line, you will find a collection of campsites reputed to be among the most remote in the entire state. Small in stature but heavyweights in Northwoods allure, Lauterman and Perch Lakes occupy space north and south of WI 70 encircled by unforgettable hiking and camping.

Perch Lake hosts five sites along the 1.3-mile loop tracing the shore, and four of those are within sight of the water; perfect for fishing/camping outings. Hot tip: The lake is packed with northern, bass, and bluegill. Lauterman Lake also offers five campsites on a 3-mile loop that include fire rings, rustic tables, and wilderness toilets. (That means just a seated perch over a hole in the ground.)

All sites are walk-in, with distances between 200 yards and a mile. The trails in the area are nearly all very well maintained, including the popular Lauterman Lake National Recreation Trail, 9 miles of sublime path through hilly forest and wetland boardwalks. Bonus points for the Whisker Lake Wilderness trailhead situated just a half mile north of Perch Lake.

The Lauterman Lake Trail treats hikers to an enchanting display of hardwood forest with a pine-spruce-fir-hemlock mix fringing the lake. Expect plenty of short, steep hills and a tougher one at the lake's south end, and a fun, winding course from start to finish.

Set off from the trailhead on a wide, hard-packed dirt path that takes a winding course through a stunning mixed forest sporting species like Norway pine, balsam fir,

A boardwalk section early on the hike.

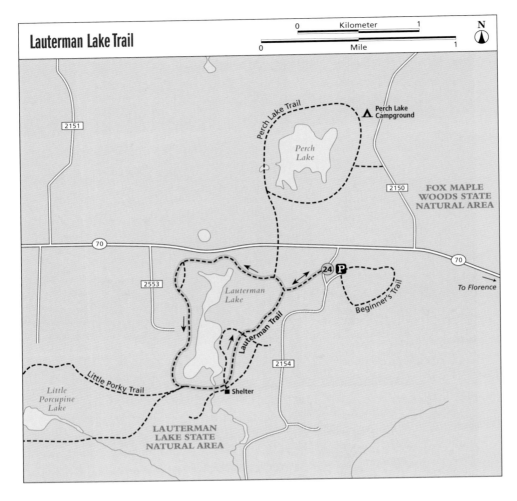

ubiquitous maple, scatterings of birch and aspen, and lots more. Overall, the trail is a mix of hilly and undulating with plenty of steeper climbs, officially a ski trail and maintained as such, so expect soggy or standing water in low sections. The counterclockwise loop passes a spur trail leading north to Perch Lake if you're up for more miles or adding another element of adventure. Follow the trail down a gradual descent to a long boardwalk through a bog area at the northern tip of the lake. You'll come upon the first of the lakeside campsites on a gentle hill above the shore. A short path leads to the water and the expected stellar views looking south.

From here, follow the path's turn to the south as it makes a couple of long, gentle S curves along the lake's western shore. Past a shelter at the south end of the lake, the path gradually moves away from the lake to return to the junction leading back to the trailhead.

Lauterman Lake cattails.

Miles and Directions

0.0 Follow the path from the trailhead into the woods across the forest road.

0.2 At the junction with the return trail, go right, following the path around the lake's northern end.

1.8 Pass the trailside shelter, heading back northeast.

3.0 Arrive back at the trailhead.

25 Perch Lake Trail

This is a great little hike in the midst of outrageous scenery and the perfect destination for remote camping only a short stroll from the trailhead.

Lake or river: Perch Lake
Photogenic factor: 4
Distance: 1.3-mile loop
Difficulty: Easy
Hiking time: About 1 hour
Trail surface: Hard-packed dirt path
Other trail users: None
Canine compatibility: Leashed pets allowed

Land status: Chequamegon-Nicolet National Forest
Fees and permits: Vehicle pass required
Maps: National forest maps; USGS Iron Mountain, MI
Trail contacts: Chequamegon-Nicolet National Forest, 500 Hansen Rd., Rhinelander 54501; (715) 362-1300; fs.usda.gov/cnnf

Finding the trailhead: From the town of Florence, follow WI 70 12.4 miles west to FR 2150. From Eagle River, follow WI 70 east 41 miles to the forest road. **Trailhead GPS:** N45 93.140' / W88 49.220'

The Hike

Accessible via a short path direct from the Lauterman Lake Trail or the forest road trailhead, Perch Lake is the perfect hike to get that way-out-there vibe, and at just over 1 mile, you can have it in an hour! The skinny, hard-packed trail follows an irregular circle around Perch Lake's shoreline, which changes shape with evolving water levels. At the southern fringe of Whisker Lake Wilderness, the trail passes through elegant mixed forest packed with the likes of birch, maple, ash, balsam fir, and red and white pine.

Whisker Lake Wilderness includes more than 7,500 acres of Northwoods elegance, although its name had a more casual origin. Old-timer locals called the grizzled trees at the shore of Whisker Lake "chin whiskers," and they still stand today, unscathed by the ravaging logging and burning of the early 1900s. The wilderness features rolling hills, wetlands, a half dozen small lakes, and three robust streams packed with trout. Fishing is especially popular at Riley and Edith Lakes and the Brule River, which traces the wilderness's northern boundary at the state line with Michigan. In addition to the Perch Lake Trail, the wilderness hosts several other paths including the Whisker Lake Trail crossing the east-to-west width of the wilderness, and about 10 additional miles of trail.

Remote camping is popular out here and allowed anywhere (camp 100 feet away from water sources), and hunting is a big hit in the fall. Be aware of hunting season dates before planning a hike outing. In winter, Whisker's wilderness trails are a dream come true for cross-country skiing.

The hike starts off with a gradual climb strewn with small boulders and then through a scoop in the ridge where it meets the start of the loop proper. The right

Winding through the Whisker Lake Wilderness.   *A bright-white birch along the trail.*

A quintessential Northwoods campsite view.

fork leads shortly to the first of Perch's five campsites, all of which are similar to this one: drop-dead gorgeous lake views, cemetery-quiet, with a tent pad, fire ring, and that incomparable Northwoods vibe.

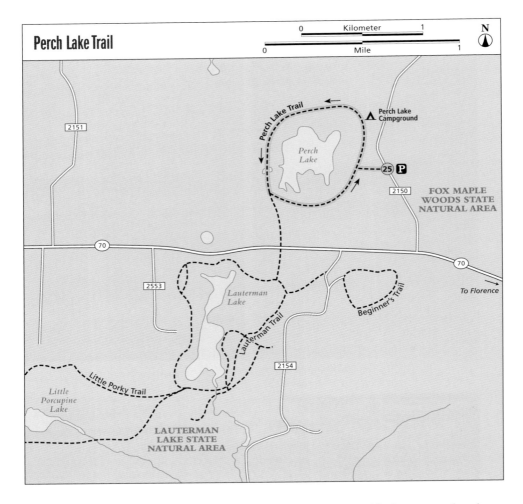

Perch Lake Trail

Following a counterclockwise direction, the trail exits a conifer-heavy stand and loops across the north side of the lake, where it drops through a shallow valley followed by a short lumpy stretch. The bottom half of the loop levels out and shoots through another narrow stand of pines before hitting the last steps to the end of the loop.

From here, simply hang a right to the trailhead.

Miles and Directions

0.0 Set off from the trailhead over a low ridge.

0.1 At the junction with the start of the loop, go right. Simply follow the loop all the way around the lake.

1.2 Return to the original trail junction and turn right.

1.3 Arrive back at the trailhead.

Door County and Lake Michigan Shoreline

Wisconsin's shape has long been likened to mittens and potholders, with their thumbs parting the waters of Green Bay and Lake Michigan. The "thumb" is formally known as the Door County Peninsula, renowned all o'er the land for its 300 miles of spectacularly beautiful shoreline, five state parks, delectable fruit orchards, diverse wildlife habitat, and lively community festivals. Speaking of thumbs, there is somewhat of a Great Mitten Debate in these parts. You see, Michigan's Lower Peninsula also looks like a mitten, but we all need two mittens to get through winter up here, right? Come to think of it, Michigan's Keweenaw Peninsula kind of looks like the beanie of a goofy winter hat, so we've got it covered.

Peninsula State Park. KENT MERHAR

Whitefish Dunes State Park. KENT MERHAR

Door County is a special place, indeed; just ask any of the more than 2 million visitors traveling here every year. They come for the cherry pie and local brews. They tour historic lighthouses ("the Door" has eleven of them!) and hike the parks. And they flock to the water with verve—on sailboats, paddleboats, or kayaks, or they just jump in! The little towns on both shores burst with character and their own unique vibe. A few of my favorites: Egg Harbor, one of America's best small towns with a classic main street and wildly talented artisans. Ephraim has Wilson's Ice Cream Parlor ('nuff said). Gills Rock is steeped in maritime history with a Norman Rockwell village flanked by high bluffs. I love Baileys Harbor for its nature preserves and peaceful beaches.

Whatever your pleasure, Door County has it and you're bound to find new adventures too. Trickling down the shoreline to the south are more must-hike lakeside parks like Point Beach and Kohler-Andrae. And don't miss Milwaukee's outdoors vibe on the Lakefront Trail or Seven Bridges Trail.

26 Newport State Park

Plan some after-dark time at Wisconsin's only designated wilderness park. Named a Dark Sky Preserve in 2017 by the International Dark Sky Association, Newport is a stargazing delight; the perfect complement to 30 miles of some of the state's best hiking trails. This pair of loop trails shows off the park's different personalities.

Lake or river: Lake Michigan
Photogenic factor: 5
Distance: 3.5-mile loop
Difficulty: Easy to moderate
Hiking time: About 90 minutes
Trail surface: Sand and cordwalk
Other trail users: None
Canine compatibility: Leashed pets allowed

Land status: State park
Fees and permits: Vehicle pass required
Maps: Park maps; USGS Spider Island and Marinette
Trail contacts: Newport State Park, 475 CR NP, Ellison Bay 54210; (920) 854-2500; dnr.wi .gov/topic/parks/name/newport

Finding the trailhead: From Ellison Bay, follow WI 42 2.3 miles east to CR NP and turn right. Go south on CR NP 2.5 miles to Newport Lane and turn right again. Follow this road 0.8 mile to the park entrance and head to the end of the park road to the trailhead. **Trailhead GPS:** N45 23.455' / W86 99.767'

The Hike

With more and more people every single day on this orb we call home, we are sadly and very rapidly losing quiet places. Places without streetlights and yard lights, without a dog barking or the drone of traffic. Places where we can look up to a sky filled with endless constellations of jewels.

The good people at the International Dark Sky Association are working to save some quiet for us today and our children tomorrow by preserving "land possessing exceptional or distinguished quality of starry nights and a protected nocturnal environment." This visionary nonprofit has designated select sites around the world as International Dark Sky Parks and Newport is Wisconsin's first.

Hiking through emerald greens. Kent Merhar

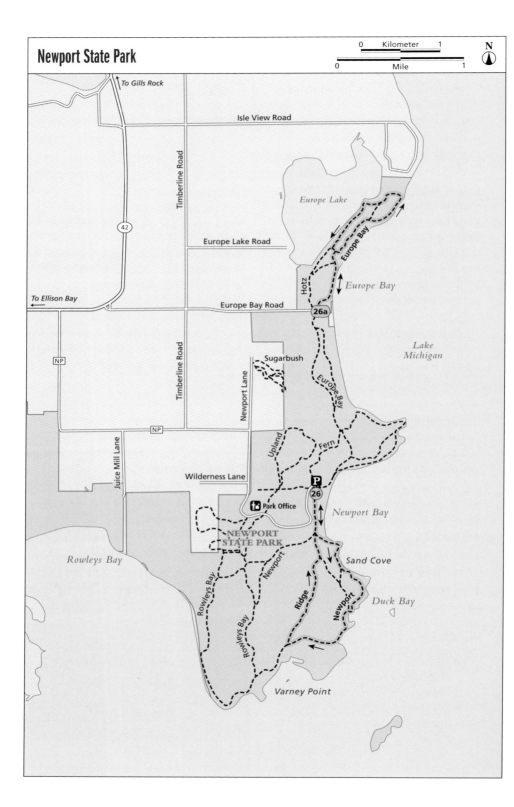

Newport State Park

To Gills Rock

Isle View Road

Timberline Road

Europe Lake

Europe Lake Road

Europe Bay

Hotz

Europe Bay Road

26a

Europe Bay

To Ellison Bay

NP

Sugarbush

Newport Lane

Timberline Road

Lake Michigan

Upland

Fern

Europe Bay

Juice Mill Lane

NP

Wilderness Lane

P
26

Park Office

Newport Bay

NEWPORT STATE PARK

Rowleys Bay

Sand Cove

Rowleys Bay

Newport

Rowleys Bay

Ridge

Newport

Duck Bay

Varney Point

0   Kilometer   1

0   Mile   1

N

Newport's designation as a wilderness park (Wisconsin's only one) makes it even better, with few paved roads or light sources and an ideal location along Lake Michigan and the northern tip of the Door Peninsula. That's music to my ears, especially with 30 miles of trails squiggling around meadows, boreal forest, and 11 miles of rugged shoreline. You can see dark skies and a star or three from anywhere in the park, but three specific locations offer especially good viewing. Check park maps for the scoop.

In addition to dark skies, Newport has sixteen primo hike-in/backpacking campsites, a swimming beach, naturalist programs, and snowshoeing and cross-country skiing in winter.

Wildflowers along the trail. KENT MERHAR

It wasn't always this rosy. When interest in the land on this part of the Door reached a heady level, the State of Wisconsin envisioned a big-revenue facility like Peninsula State Park with heavy day use and a huge campground. The locals were vociferously opposed, fought the proposal, and won. That victory led to our first wilderness state park, which keeps the area in its most natural state. Development is not allowed, so our children and theirs will see this wonderful place just as it is today.

To experience it best, hike the trail, and away we go. From the trailhead, the path hugs close to the squiggly shoreline along Sand Cove. Phenomenal views appear from openings in the forest as the trail curves around a stub of land on the way to Duck Bay. A trio of to-die-for campsites are situated along this stretch, and there's another deeper in the woods. I highly recommend spending a night or two out here.

A short track west leads to the topside of the Newport Ridge Trail and the option to check out the views from Varney Point and extend the loop south and north along part of Rowleys Bay. Today, however, turn back northeast here and hike through the quiet conifer-hardwood forest toward the Sand Cove junction and the homestretch to the trailhead.

Miles and Directions

0.0 Hike south from the trailhead, branching left along the shore where the Newport Trail continues south.

1.4 At the junction with the Newport Trail, turn left.

2.1 At the junction with the Ridge Trail, turn right and follow the Ridge and Newport Trails back to the trailhead.

3.5 Arrive back at the trailhead.

26a Europe Lake Loop

See map on page 108.
Lake or river: Lake Michigan, Europe Bay, and Europe Lake
Photogenic factor: 5

Distance: 3.0-mile lollipop loop
Difficulty: Easy to moderate
Hiking time: About 75 minutes
Trail surface: Sand, packed dirt, and cordwalk

Finding the trailhead: From the state park office, head back north on Newport Lane to CR NP and go west 0.5 mile to Timberline Road. Turn right and head north again 1 mile to Europe Bay Road. Turn right and find the trailhead in 1.1 miles at Liberty Grove Town Park. The trail starts at the road and goes north. **Trailhead GPS:** N45 25.942' / W86 98.600'

The Hike

Starting from Liberty Grove Town Park, this short loopy hike follows the thin strip of land between Lake Michigan and Europe Lake, passing along sand dunes and seagrass on its earliest sections and then into the woods. Other than slight undulations in terra firma, the trail remains largely flat. (Expect somewhat hillier sections on the return Hotz Trail.)

Lake Michigan on the Europe Bay loop. KENT MERHAR

At the trail's northern end, you'll loop to the eastern shore of camel-shaped Europe Lake and finish the loop southbound back to Europe Bay Road and the trailhead. Want more miles? Get seven of them by starting from the main park area or adding the loop south of the Liberty trailhead.

Hot tip: Europe Lake's maximum depth is only 10 feet. That means it warms up quickly and is great for swimming or floating a canoe.

Miles and Directions

0.0   Hike north on the Europe Bay Trail in the woods, paralleling the shoreline.

1.0   At the junction with the Hotz Trail, turn right. The trail hugs the shore and then reconnects with the Europe Bay Trail. Follow Europe Bay back south and get back on the Hotz Trail.

1.6   Turn right at Hotz, round a bulbous peninsula, and hike south, close to the shore of Europe Bay.

2.2   Turn left here.

2.3   Turn right back on the Europe Bay Trail for the return.

3.0   Arrive back at the trailhead.

THE DARK OF NIGHT

The International Dark Sky Association is the world's oldest organization dedicated to pre-serving our dark sky heritage. IDA was founded in 1988 and since then has made an enor-mous impact on keeping dark skies the way they're supposed to be. The dedicated group helped make places like Newport possible, and they continue to lead the way away from the light. Don't miss their info-packed website at www.darksky.org.

27 Peninsula State Park—Nicolet Loop

Get a twofer at this spectacularly beautiful park on the Green Bay side of the Door Peninsula. A pair of loop trails serves up stop-in-your-tracks views, rugged and easy-going hiking, and an 1860s lighthouse.

Lake or river: Nicolet Bay
Photogenic factor: 5+
Distance: 3.8-mile loop, with many options for additional miles
Difficulty: Mix of easy to difficult
Hiking time: 90 minutes to 2 hours
Trail surface: Hard-packed dirt
Other trail users: None

Canine compatibility: Leashed pets allowed
Land status: State park
Fees and permits: Vehicle pass required
Maps: Park maps; USGS Ephraim
Trail contacts: Peninsula State Park, 9462 Shore Rd., Fish Creek 54212; (920) 868-3258; dnr.wi.gov/topic/parks/name/peninsula/

Finding the trailhead: From Sturgeon Bay, follow WI 42 22 miles north to the village of Fish Creek. The main park entrance is just east of town, but continue on WI 42 3 miles to the eastern entry at Shore Road. Turn left and follow Shore Road 1 mile north and take the Eagle Terrace fork to the right. The parking area and trailhead are 0.1 mile farther on the left.
Trailhead GPS: N45 16.081' / W87 19.532'

The Hike

The first hunter-gatherer clans that lived in this area 11,000 years ago knew a good thing when they saw it. Today's Peninsula State Park is otherworldly gorgeous and chock-full of cover-shot scenic sights. How does this sound? Eight miles of shoreline; high, rocky bluffs; a vertical cedar forest; and a who's who of wildlife species. Did I mention Peninsula boasts two of Wisconsin's State Natural Areas? The White Cedar Forest and Beech Maple Forest SNAs are loaded with all manner of flora and fauna providing critical habitats and research environments. Throw in sandy beaches and wildly popular summer theater performances and Peninsula checks all the boxes.

This is Wisconsin's second state park, established in 1909, and after a slow but gradual start, the park became a go-to destination for the outdoors-minded. Door County Days, a summer festival with picnics, music, and sports, attracted thousands and the park soon transformed into one of the Midwest's premier active-interest locations. Today it is known as Wisconsin's most complete, albeit crowded, park—nearly 500 campsites, group camps, outdoor theater, golf course, beach, miles of trails, and a lighthouse. Plenty for everyone, that's for sure.

Feel like taking it easy? Stroll along the Sunset Trail near Eagle Bluff Lighthouse for life-list views of Green Bay and a cluster of islands to the west. For a more rugged day out, head east to the Sentinel and Eagle Trails. Whatever your pleasure, you'll find it here.

Nicolet Bay and Horseshoe Island. DENICE BREAUX

And you won't be alone. Peninsula's list of critters includes seldom-seen crustaceans, globally rare snails, and unique ferns living in microhabitats in the park's cliffs. Larger and more mobile species are plentiful here as well, such as white-tailed deer, foxes, porcupines, grouse, turkey, and rabbits. In the trees and overhead are roughly 125 species of birds like warblers, orioles, bluebirds, cardinals, and raptors of various ilk.

This is indeed a very active place and not just aboveground. The cliffs at Peninsula are part of the expansive Niagara Escarpment, a limestone ridge stretching across nearly all of Wisconsin, part of Ontario, Canada, and on to the netherworld beneath Niagara Falls. Impressive, especially considering the escarpment started out as plain ol' mud at the bottom of an enormous saltwater sea that covered this area. The ridge took shape about 430 million years ago and today provides the launch pad for the mighty Niagara Falls.

This hike sets off from the Eagle Terrace parking area and does a little duckbill loop before tracing the ridge along the shoreline of Nicolet Bay. Enjoy breathtaking views of the bay and Horseshoe Island as the path drops down close to the shore to the Minnehaha Trail, then makes a steady climb south with one steep section back up to the top of the ridge. The Lone Pine Trail takes you through resplendent northern mesic forest of maple, beech, aspen, and scattered conifers, connecting with the Sentinel Trail.

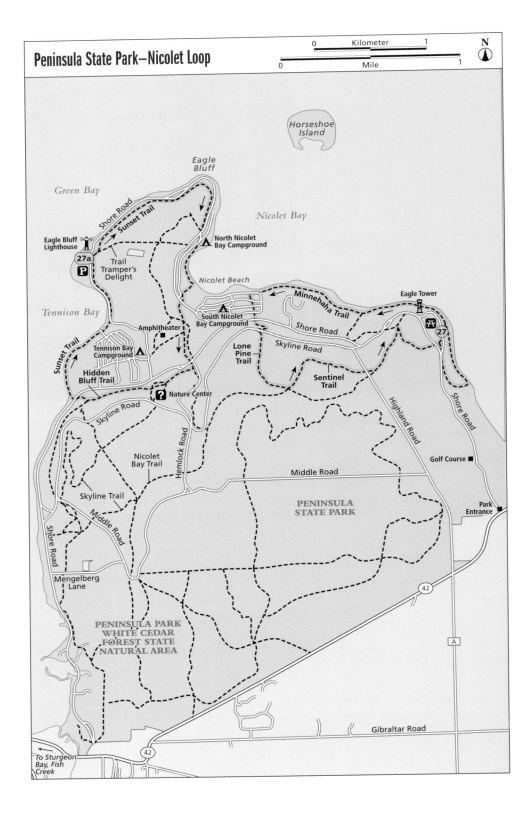

Peninsula State Park–Nicolet Loop

Kilometer
0 1
Mile
0 1

N

Horseshoe Island

Eagle Bluff

Green Bay

Nicolet Bay

Shore Road

Sunset Trail

Eagle Bluff Lighthouse

27a
P

Trail Tramper's Delight

North Nicolet Bay Campground

Nicolet Beach

Minnehaha Trail

Eagle Tower

27

Tennison Bay

Sunset Trail

Amphitheater

South Nicolet Bay Campground

Shore Road

Tennison Bay Campground

Lone Pine Trail

Skyline Road

Sentinel Trail

Hidden Bluff Trail

Nature Center

Skyline Road

Hemlock Road

Nicolet Bay Trail

Highland Road

Golf Course

Skyline Trail

Middle Road

PENINSULA STATE PARK

Shore Road

Middle Road

Park Entrance

Mengelberg Lane

42

PENINSULA PARK WHITE CEDAR FOREST STATE NATURAL AREA

A

Gibraltar Road

42

To Sturgeon Bay, Fish Creek

Splendid view of Nicolet Bay. DENICE BREAUX

Follow Sentinel on an easy climb back across Highland Road to return to the trailhead. Note that a couple sections of this loop travel over mildly challenging (fun) terrain of rocks and roots.

Miles and Directions

0.0 From the trailhead, follow the Eagle Trail signs and hike briefly southeast, looping back north along the shore.

1.0 At the junction with the Minnehaha Trail, turn right.

1.6 At the junction with Lone Pine Trail, turn left.

2.4 At the junction with Sentinel Trail, turn left.

3.3 At the junction with Eagle Trail, turn right.

3.8 Arrive at the trailhead.

27a Sunset Loop

See map on page 114.

Lake or river: Green Bay and Tennison Bay
Photogenic factor: 5+
Distance: 3.8-mile loop, with many options for additional miles

Difficulty: Moderate
Hiking time: 90 minutes to 2 hours
Trail surface: Hard-packed dirt and paved

Finding the trailhead: From Sturgeon Bay, follow WI 42 22 miles north to the village of Fish Creek. The main park entrance is just east of town at Shore Road. Turn left and follow Shore Road 3.1 miles to the Eagle Bluff Lighthouse parking area on the left. The trail starts adjacent to the entrance road. **Trailhead GPS:** N45 16.811' / W87 23.634'

The Hike

My list of all-time favorite hikes is long enough for a book of its own, and this one ranks way up there, starting with drop-dead gorgeous views at the Eagle Bluff Lighthouse. Ogle the picture-perfect scene with a backdrop of Adventure, Little Strawberry, Jack, and Pirate Islands, and then pry yourself away to start the hike.

Follow the paved Sunset Trail along Shore Road and around Eagle Bluff, descending gradually past Nicolet Bay and then back up across the park road and into the woods. A right turn at Hidden Bluff Trail leads through more of the same ridiculously beautiful forest as the Nicolet hike and just south of the White Cedar Nature Reserve. The reserve's visitor center is nestled among the aroma of its namesake trees and is loaded with historic photos, park info, and gift items. This building was originally constructed in 1939 and was used as a warming house for the fearless crowd attempting the nearby ski jump and revelers at the toboggan run. Both sites were later abandoned, but the stories live on.

From the nature reserve, the trail descends easily to the water again and then along Tennison Bay to one final easy rise to the trailhead. Don't forget that the entire Sunset Trail is just over 9 miles and offers a full day of invigorating outdoor fun.

THE VERTICAL FOREST

The giant trees of the Pacific Northwest have some stiff competition in Wisconsin. The ancient white cedars growing in the "vertical forest" of Door County's Niagara Escarpment are grizzled and wise, latched onto solid rock for centuries. The stalwart trees sprouted from tiny fissures in sheer rock faces and escaped the ravages of logging, agriculture, and rampant development. At Ontario's Bruce Peninsula, a team of scientists discovered cedars just 10 feet tall and a foot in diameter that are more than 1,000 years old.

The Sunset Trail. KENT MERHAR

Miles and Directions

0.0　From the trailhead, set off hiking northbound on the Sunset Trail adjacent to Shore Road, and loop around Eagle Bluff. Follow the Sunset Trail signs across the park road and continue past Nicolet Bay.

1.8　Cross Bluff Road and go right at Hidden Bluff Trail, hiking back toward the water.

2.7　Turn right at the Sunset Trail junction.

3.8　Arrive back at the trailhead.

28 Whitefish Dunes State Park

How's this for a day out? Nearly 900 acres of aged forest on 3 miles of rugged Lake Michigan shoreline and Wisconsin's highest sand dunes. Come out and roam.

Lake or river: Lake Michigan
Photogenic factor: 5
Distance: 2.8-mile loop, with options for additional miles
Difficulty: Easy
Hiking time: About 75 minutes
Trail surface: Hard-packed dirt and sand dunes
Other trail users: None

Canine compatibility: Leashed pets allowed
Land status: State park
Fees and permits: Vehicle pass required
Maps: Park maps; USGS Jacksonport
Trail contacts: Whitefish Dunes State Park, 3275 Clark Lake Rd., Sturgeon Bay 54235; (920) 823-2400; dnr.wi.gov/topic/parks/name/whitefish/

Finding the trailhead: From Sturgeon Bay, follow WI 42/57 north 2.7 miles to the split, and then WI 57 north 5.9 miles to Clark Lake Road. Turn right and follow Clark Lake Road 3.8 miles to the park entrance. The trailhead is adjacent to the nature center. **Trailhead GPS:** N44 92.724' / W87 18.297'

The Hike

Did you know that the land of today's Whitefish Dunes State Park has evidence of human settling as far back as 100 BC? That's a long time ago, and other peoples settled here at no less than seven other time periods up to the late 1800s.

What drew consistent groups of people to this place? Much of it is due to the great abundance of fish like lake sturgeon, whitefish, walleye, and trout, as well as plants for food and medicine. Indeed, many rare plant species lived here in the earliest days and still do today, a fact that spurred 1930 conservationists to protect the dunes area from development.

And we are very glad they did because today one can walk along the peaceful quiet of the dunes and see tracks of foxes and deer, or spot a muskrat or rabbit or even an elusive black bear. While most of the park's land-based wildlife only occasionally reveal themselves, scat, bones, and tracks are common sights.

Visitors are more likely to see and hear birds overhead and in the forested areas, grassy dunes, and wetlands and at the shoreline. And what an avian lineup it is, including the likes of Canada warbler, osprey, least flycatcher, black-throated blue and green warbler, and many others. Wetland areas are home to vibrant populations of amphibians such as wood frogs, spring peepers, chorus frogs, toads, salamanders, and turtles.

Flora at Whitefish is no less dramatic than the critters, with rare species like thick-spike wheatgrass, prairie sand reed, and Wisconsin's largest population of the threatened dune thistle. Vibrant flowers live here as well. On your hike look for dune goldenrod, dwarf lake iris, and sand reed grass.

The beach, of course, is the big geographic draw, and like its enormous Saharan relative, the dunes at Whitefish are constantly in motion, forever at the mercy of nature's hand. Winds bellowing in from across Lake Michigan blast against the shore, lift up the sand grain by grain, and move it inland. This action eventually forms a dune. The wind then drops down the steep back slope of the dune, picks up more sand, and builds another dune.

The whole thing is like an eternal highlight reel of nature in action and makes this hike all the more enjoyable. The Red Trail takes hikers southwest from the nature center into the woods along the lakeshore. A couple of beach-access points take you to the water's edge and along the dunes. About halfway through the hike, you will reach the junction with the Old Baldy Trail. Don't miss this short side trip along a boardwalk and up a set of stairs to the park's highest point at 93 feet above lake level. There's an observation deck up there and outrageous views of Lake Michigan, Clark Lake, and a big chunk of the rest of the park.

From Baldy, the Red Trail mingles with the Green and Yellow on a squiggly path back to the trailhead.

The cordwalk trail along the dunes above Lake Michigan. KENT MERHAR

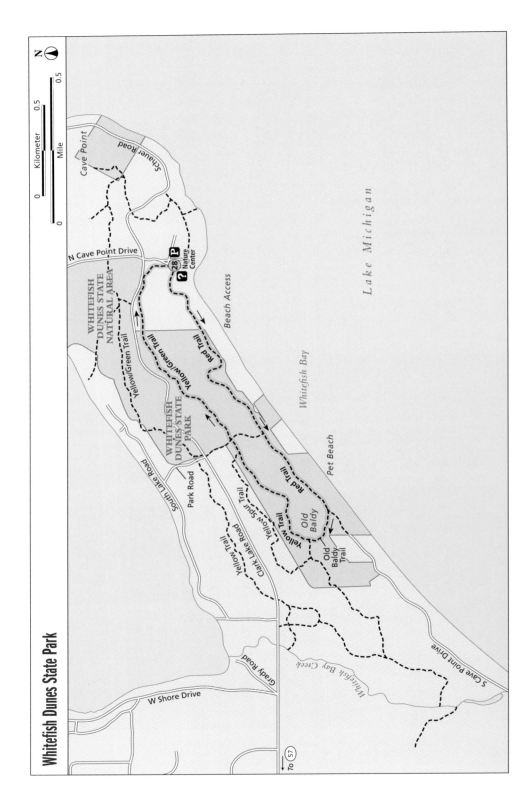

Whitefish Dunes State Park

Whitefish Dunes State Park

Whitefish Dunes State Natural Area

Whitefish Dunes State Park

Cave Point

Schauer Road

N Cave Point Drive

Nature Center

Beach Access

Red Trail

Yellow/Green Trail

Yellow/Green Trail

South Lake Road

Park Road

Clark Lake Road

Yellow Trail

Yellow Spur

Yellow Trail

Red Trail

Old Baldy

Old Baldy Trail

Pet Beach

Whitefish Bay

Lake Michigan

W Shore Drive

Grady Road

Whitefish Bay Creek

S Cave Point Drive

To 57

N

Kilometer

Mile

0   0.5

0   0.5

28

Miles and Directions

0.0 From the trailhead, follow the Red Trail southwesterly from the nature center, almost immediately passing a beach-access trail.

0.7 Pass another beach-access trail.

1.3 At the junction with Old Baldy Trail, head up the trail and stairs for great views from the top. Loop back on the Yellow and Green Trails to return to the trailhead.

2.8 Arrive back at the trailhead.

DUNE PEOPLE

From 100 BC to AD 300 the Whitefish Dunes area was occupied by its earliest settlers, the North Bay people. Their territory extended from Green Bay to Rock Island, within which there were likely several separate but interacting bands that traveled the shores of the peninsula by canoe. These people were skilled in pottery craft, and archaeologists have discovered much evidence among the dunes. It is believed the North Bay people only lived here in the spring and summer, probably arriving for spring sturgeon fishing and staying to midsummer. Then what? Did they winter in Phoenix?

The Heins Creek people descended from the North Bay groups, occupying the shores of the Door Peninsula in a large population, supported through fishing. The Heins Creek lived here to about AD 750.

The next occupation was the Woodland people, from AD 800 to AD 900. By now, a good-sized village had been established and bustled with activity from spring to fall, with winter seeing the departure of the population to winter hunting camps on the Green Bay side or inland wetland areas.

The Oneota people arrived in this area around AD 900 and were likely descendants of the later Woodland groups. The Oneota introduced agriculture to their lives, in addition to traditional hunting and fishing. Corn and squash were popular; the former probably ground to flour to make dough. One archaeological dig uncovered a pit oven with fire-hardened dolomite.

29 Potawatomi State Park

One of Wisconsin's state park gems, Potawatomi boasts rolling, emerald-green valleys complemented with raggedy limestone cliffs and ridiculously gorgeous views of Sturgeon Bay.

Lake or river: Sturgeon Bay
Photogenic factor: 5
Distance: 2.6-mile loop, with options for additional miles
Difficulty: Easy
Hiking time: About 75 minutes
Trail surface: Hard-packed dirt
Other trail users: None

Canine compatibility: Leashed pets allowed
Land status: State park
Fees and permits: Vehicle pass required
Maps: Park maps; USGS Sturgeon Bay West
Trail contacts: Potawatomi State Park, 3740 CR PD, Sturgeon Bay 54235; (920) 746-2890; dnr.wi.gov/topic/parks/name/potawatomi/

Finding the trailhead: From Green Bay at I-43, follow WI 57 north 36 miles to Park Drive (CR PD). Turn left and head north 2.4 miles to the park entrance. From the entrance station, follow South Norway Road 1 mile to a parking area on the right. Find the trail at the north end.
Trailhead GPS: N44 85.377' / W87 40.387'

The Hike

I always feel a deep sense of vicarious pride and often walk with thoughts drifting to a time long past when I'm here at this magical place. The Native American tribe who once called this land home were known as Bo-De-Wad-Me—"keeper of the fire." They lived in a land of rugged cliffs and forests high above the bay, among the gulls and terns, songbirds and deer.

The state park we see today retains much of that mystique and spirit. Dense forest of maple, birch, basswood, and red and white pine blanket a blend of sweeping valleys and short rocky hills and knobs. Among the trees live a host of wild critters. White-tailed deer are all over, along with foxes, squirrels, raccoons, turtles, and waterfowl. Well over 200 species of songbirds of various ilk live in or migrate through the park,

DOOR COUNTY'S STONE FLEET

Door County's first industry, a limestone quarry, started in 1834 at Government Bluff, 150 feet above Sturgeon Bay. The original plan was to use the stone to build a military fort, but that never came to pass. The federal government, however, used the stone to build piers and harbors around Lake Michigan. By 1898 four more quarries were built and supplied stone to construct nearly every pier and breakwater around the lake.

The rustic Hemlock Trail. DENICE BREAUX

Dreamy views of Sturgeon Bay. DENICE BREAUX

and you can see herring gulls, ring-billed gulls, and terns riding the thermals along the cliff-side shoreline.

This hike along the Hemlock Trail takes in much of those highlights, starting right off the bat by sharing double billing with the Ice Age Trail along the cliff top above Sturgeon Bay. In fact, the IAT's eastern terminus is just a short way south of this hike's starting point. Views of the bay appear through intermittent breaks in the trees and soon you are treated to a linger-worthy overlook of Cabot Point, the mainland far across the bay, and faraway views of Green Bay to the northwest. Unforgettable.

Spring cherry blossoms. DENICE BREAUX

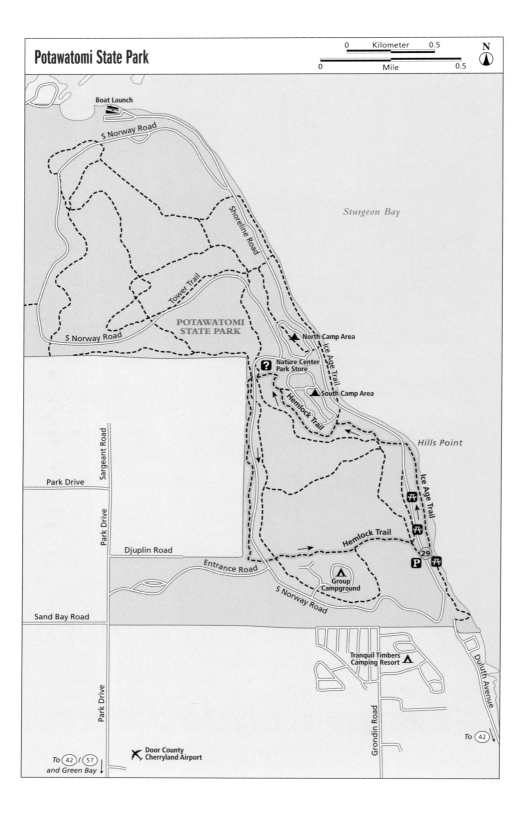

Potawatomi State Park

0 — Kilometer — 0.5
0 — Mile — 0.5

N

Boat Launch

S Norway Road

Shoreline Road

Sturgeon Bay

Tower Trail

S Norway Road

POTAWATOMI
STATE PARK

North Camp Area

Ice Age Trail

Nature Center-
Park Store

South Camp Area

Hemlock Trail

Hills Point

Ice Age Trail

Sargeant Road

Park Drive

Park Drive

Djuplin Road

Hemlock Trail

29

P

Entrance Road

S Norway Road

Group
Campground

Sand Bay Road

Park Drive

Tranquil Timbers
Camping Resort

Grondin Road

Duluth Avenue

To 42

Door County
Cherryland Airport

To 42 / 57
and Green Bay

Stone steps in the woods. DENICE BREAUX

Near Hills Point the path crosses the park road and makes a short, steep climb away from the water and into thick woods. In a short bit the IAT splits off and continues northwest while the Hemlock Trail takes a gradual curve past the campground area and nature center.

Cross the road again and begin heading due south, paralleling the road to your left. The trail stays mostly flat along this section, crosses the road once again, and then travels over barely there hills to a final downhill coast to the trailhead.

Got some extra time? The Ancient Shorelines Nature Trail is a don't-miss park highlight, and the Tower Trail treats hikers to its namesake, 75-foot observation tower with a 180-degree view of Sawyer Harbor. On clear days you can see 16 miles across Green Bay. Nice! And don't forget about the park's pair of campgrounds with well over one hundred campsites. Winter camping (*brrrr*) is popular here as well, as is cross-country skiing, sledding, and snowshoeing.

Miles and Directions

0.0 From the trailhead, set off hiking northbound along the shoreline.

0.8 Reach the Hills Point area. Cross the road and continue on the trail.

1.0 Ice Age Trail splits here and continues north. Veer left and follow the path past the campground areas.

1.4 Cross the road again, curve left, and hike due south, paralleling the road.

2.3 Another road crossing.

2.6 Arrive back at the trailhead.

30 Point Beach State Forest

Six miles of Lake Michigan beach, 11 miles of hiking trails, and an active US Coast Guard lighthouse. This loop traces the shoreline and an ancient dune ridge.

Lake or river: Lake Michigan
Photogenic factor: 5
Distance: 4.6-mile loop
Difficulty: Easy
Hiking time: About 1 hour 45 minutes
Trail surface: Hard-packed dirt
Other trail users: Mountain bikers

Canine compatibility: Leashed pets allowed
Land status: State forest
Fees and permits: Vehicle pass required
Maps: Park maps; USGS Two Rivers
Trail contacts: Point Beach State Forest, 9400 CR O, Two Rivers 54241; (920) 794-7480; dnr .wi.gov/topic/parks/name/pointbeach/

Finding the trailhead: From WI 42 in Two Rivers, follow CR O 4.7 miles north to the park entrance road. Follow this road 0.3 mile to the parking area and trailhead.
Trailhead GPS: N44 21.132' / W87 50.990'

The Hike

After the time of American Indian residence here during the Copper Culture age, including Winnebago, Sauk, Fox, Miami, and Potawatomi, a settler named Peter Rowley moved in and set up a trading post. He decided to name the place Mink River, but when surveyors scouted the area in the mid-1800s, they had never heard of the Mink River name. They knew of Rowley, however, and renamed the location after him (changing the spelling a few years later to Rawley Point).

A robust hemlock population here spurred the establishment of many tanneries, such as the Wisconsin Leather Company. Hemlock is a main ingredient for making leather, and for close to four decades this was the highlight industry in the Two Rivers area.

Much of the final end product from the leather trade was transported by steamers and schooners, and Lake Michigan was busy with vessels navigating its challenging waters. Some ships unfortunately didn't make it to the next port. Shipwrecks are common throughout the Great Lakes, and one of Lake Michigan's most notable was the steamer *Vernon*, which sank 200 feet in an area less than a dozen miles northeast of Two Rivers. The ship settled upright on the lake bottom and remains upright today, making it a huge hit with divers.

Another famous wreck was the *Rouse Simmons*, popularly known as the Christmas Tree Ship. Every year, two brothers from Michigan filled the *Rouse* with Christmas trees to bring to Chicago. Alas, the ship disappeared in a harsh 1912 storm and only a few washed-ashore trees remained until a diver discovered the wreck in 1971, still packed with hundreds of trees complete with their needles perfectly preserved.

Shoreside Lake Michigan views. DENICE BREAUX

Reports differ on why the ship sank but some put the onus on the enormous load of trees that didn't allow the ship to ride at an optimal level.

Terrestrial-based features of Point Beach State Forest include its three State Natural Areas. Wilderness Ridge SNA is dominated by a ridge–swale environment with nearly thirty species of sedges and dozens more of grasses. Two Creeks Buried Forest SNA is just north of the state forest and includes 11,000-year-old sediment layers. Point Beach Ridges SNA is home to swales and ridges and the endangered sand dune willow.

Start this hike from the lighthouse area and head south on the Ice Age Trail. The trail meanders along, alternating between the beach and a grove of white cedar woods, with a couple enticing boardwalk access trails and beachside benches. The trail passes directly over the dunes, with sights and sounds of Lake Michigan right off your left shoulder. Hike past the indoor group camp cabins, and in short order Molash Creek appears beyond the pines, with a bench conveniently located for viewing this idyllic scene.

From here, connect with the Ridges Trail. This section of the hike makes a beeline back northeast through resplendent forest of maple, ash, beech, birch, aspen, red and white pine, and scattered hemlock.

Before long the path connects with the Blue Loop and returns to the trailhead.

FINAL VOYAGE

On January 15, 1885, the tug *Boss* was moored securely to a dock in Two Rivers. The next morning it was missing. A fierce winter storm was in the works and many people thought the tug broke its lines and drifted out into the lake. Others guessed it was cast adrift or even stolen. The tug was found in the spring of 1887 about 4 miles south of Two Rivers.

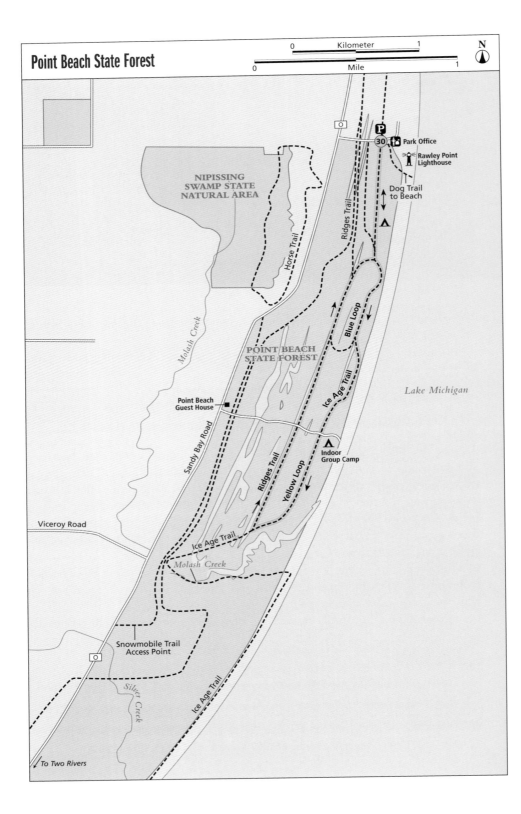

Point Beach State Forest

Kilometer
0   1
0   Mile   1

N

NIPISSING SWAMP STATE NATURAL AREA

Horse Trail

Molash Creek

Ridges Trail

Park Office

Rawley Point Lighthouse

Dog Trail to Beach

Blue Loop

POINT BEACH STATE FOREST

Ice Age Trail

Lake Michigan

Point Beach Guest House

Sandy Bay Road

Ridges Trail

Yellow Loop

Indoor Group Camp

Viceroy Road

Ice Age Trail

Molash Creek

Snowmobile Trail Access Point

Silver Creek

Ice Age Trail

To Two Rivers

Boardwalk trail toward the lake. DENICE BREAUX

Hiking a wide trail in the woods. DENICE BREAUX

Miles and Directions

0.0 From the trailhead, hike due south on the trail adjacent to parking area's entrance. This will connect to the Ice Age Trail. Follow the IAT southbound along the shore.

2.5 At the junction with the Ridges Trail, turn right.

3.8 Turn right here for the final few dozen steps of the Blue Loop. Turn left on the IAT and proceed straight ahead on the trail back to the trailhead.

4.6 Arrive at the trailhead.

31 Horicon National Wildlife Refuge

Horicon Marsh is a Big Deal. It's one of the country's largest freshwater marshes, a Wetland of International Importance, and a State and Global Important Bird Area. Lofty credentials indeed, and this is the place to be to get your wildlife fix.

Lake or river: Horicon Marsh
Photogenic factor: 4+
Distance: 1.4-mile loop
Difficulty: Easy
Hiking time: About 1 hour
Trail surface: Mix of hard-packed dirt, chipped, and grassy
Other trail users: None

Canine compatibility: Leashed pets allowed
Land status: US Fish and Wildlife Service
Fees and permits: None
Maps: DNR maps; USGS Mayville South
Trail contacts: Horicon National Wildlife Refuge, W4279 Headquarters Rd., Mayville 53050; (920) 387-2658; www.fws.gov/refuge/horicon/

Finding the trailhead: The little town of Horicon is roughly 25 miles southwest of Fond du Lac. From East Lake Street in Horicon, head north on North Palmatory Street 1 mile to the parking area and trailhead. **Trailhead GPS:** N43 46.624' / W88 62.135'

The Hike

Horicon Marsh is nothing less than spectacular. This is real life-list stuff and should be way up on your hiking must-do list. Well over 33,000 acres, the marsh (the largest freshwater cattail marsh in the United States) is critical habitat for more than 300 species of birds, far too many to even begin to list here, as well as other critters like red foxes, frogs, toads, bats, muskrat, fish, and turtles.

But did you know that this area was once a veritable wasteland, nearly completely devoid of wildlife? After the Canada goose population was nearly wiped out, attempts were made to dredge the marsh for farmland. Thankfully those attempts failed and today the geese are back in great numbers, along with a celebrity list of other bird life.

Horicon Marsh was established in 1941 to set aside a sanctuary for migratory birds and waterfowl and as a peaceful place for people to come and connect with this special natural world. A highlight of the refuge is more than 15,000 acres of marsh habitat made of dense expanses of cattail, sedges, bulrushes, and burreed. That all means excellent food and habitat for all manner of ducks and local and migrating birds. Indeed, fall migration around here is like the World's Fair of bird life, with a huge amount of avian activity from the likes of sandhill cranes, great blue herons, Canada geese, cormorants, and raptors.

Bird-watching is, of course, wildly popular here, and the flat terrain makes it easy to move around and get the best look of your favorites. In fact, don't be surprised to spot upwards of one hundred different bird species in a single day! The visitor center

Wide-open marshland. KENT MERHAR

is packed with extensive beta as well, including interactive video tours and more background history on area bird life than you've likely ever seen in one place.

Out on the trails you'll find overlook points that offer faraway views of the marsh's most stunning attributes. For this hike, start from the southern parking area on Palmatory Street and wander north on the Quick's Point Trail. This loop trail first leads through a stand of mixed hardwoods and then out into a mix of gently rolling and level terrain, much of it covered in gloriously wild meadows filled with all manner of native grasses and wildflowers. Great views of the western marshlands unfurl from the tops of the low hills, and one particular stretch of the trail reminds me of an old

HORICON'S HERONS

Poking out of Horicon's marshy wetlands is a handful of islands like land-based versions of icebergs. The islands are actually the tops of buried glacial drumlins from the last ice age. The largest is Fourmile Island, a critical SNA recently hosting Wisconsin's largest heron and egret rookery. Upwards of 1,000 heron and egret pairs nested here, including the great blue heron, great egret, double-crested cormorant, and black-crowned night heron. Overpopulation of the birds and a catastrophic storm severely degraded this habitat, but the birds still nest here, albeit in much lower numbers.

Lake view from a hilltop trail. KENT MERHAR

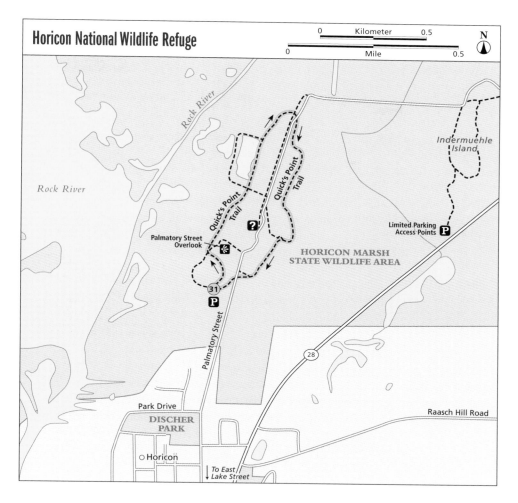

wagon trail crossing empty lands of the plains. Expect to see plenty of the refuge's resident wildlife along this stretch as well, frolicking in their watery or woodsy habitats.

At the top end of the loop, the path wanders through another woodland and then turns south, passing the lake adjacent to Indermuehle Island and scattered patches of wetland back to the trailhead.

Miles and Directions

0.0   From the trailhead, hike through the woods and out into open land near the marsh.

0.7   At the junction with the top of the loop, follow the path straight ahead, leading toward the lake. Continue southwest back to the trailhead.

1.4   Arrive back at the trailhead.

32 High Cliff State Park

Get elevated, drop-dead gorgeous views of Wisconsin's largest inland lake on this feature-packed hike, including Indian mounds and old lime kiln ruins.

Lake or river: Lake Winnebago
Photogenic factor: 4+
Distance: 2.2-mile loop with lots of additional available mileage
Difficulty: Easy
Hiking time: About 90 minutes
Trail surface: Hard-packed dirt
Other trail users: None

Canine compatibility: Leashed pets allowed
Land status: State park
Fees and permits: Vehicle pass required
Maps: Park maps; USGS Sherwood
Trail contacts: High Cliff State Park, N7630 State Park Rd., Sherwood 54169; (920) 989-1106; dnr.wi.gov/topic/parks/name/highcliff

Finding the trailhead: From the eastern fringe of the little town of Sherwood at WI 55, follow Clifton Road (becomes Spring Hill Drive) 1.6 miles to the park entrance. Past the entrance, turn left at Lower Cliff Road and go 0.7 mile to High Cliff Road. Turn left again and follow this road 0.7 mile to the last parking area on your left. The Red Bird Trail starts at the western end of the lot. **Trailhead GPS:** N44 16.283' / W88 28.669'

The Hike

Within Wisconsin's borders, Lake Winnebago is the state's largest lake, stretching 31 miles north to south and roughly 7 miles wide. It's a big ol' lake and attracts legions of water-loving fans on all manner of boats or paddling along in canoes and kayaks, with great views of the rugged limestone cliffs rising 40 feet above the eastern shore, making up part of the Niagara Escarpment, the immense limestone band stretching from Wisconsin to its namesake falls in New York. This fascinating geological wonder is made of countless layers of limestone sediment deposited here millions of years ago. The park itself boasts more than a mile of wildly scenic shoreline (with its own marina) and is home to red foxes, deer, woodchucks, warblers, and an active population of purple martins.

The park is also steeped in human history, dating back 1,500 years to nomadic Indians who built still-visible effigy mounds in the shapes of animals such as panthers, buffalo, and bears, or geometric shapes including conical and lineal. The much more recent years of the late 1800s to mid-1900s were very lively times in the company town of Clifton, made up of worker housing, a store, telegraph office, and, of course, a tavern. The Western Lime and Cement Company owned the town, and product extracted from the quarry was shipped all over the Midwest for use in cement, brick mortar, and gravel. Today the old store is a museum and park where visitors can see the kiln ruins and hike the historic Lime Kiln Trail.

Lake Winnebago views from the Red Bird Trail. DENICE BREAUX

For a highlight reel of the park's best, beeline to the Red Bird Trail, marked at the trailhead with an impressive statue of Red Bird, a Winnebago tribe leader and peacemaker with early settlers. Close to the statue is another area landmark: a wooden observation tower that takes you 40 feet in the air for outrageous views of the lake and bucolic Wisconsin countryside.

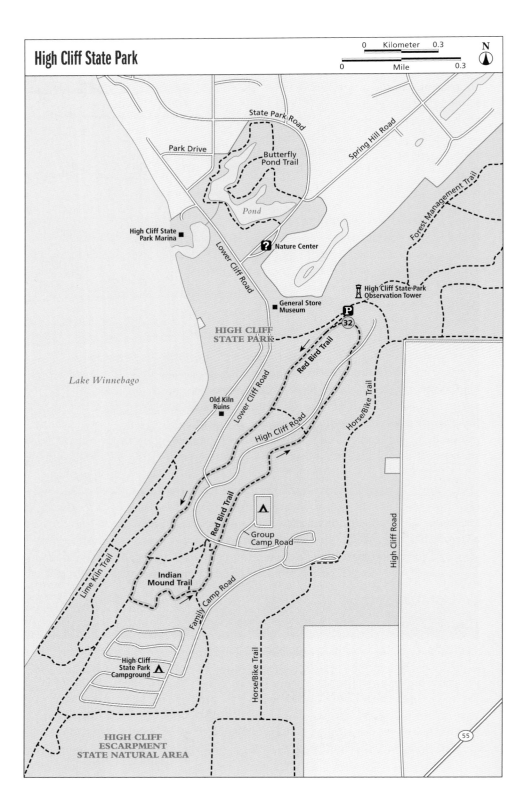

0   Kilometer   0.3

0   Mile   0.3

N

State Park Road

Spring Hill Road

Park Drive

Butterfly
Pond Trail

Pond

Forest Management Trail

High Cliff State
Park Marina

Lower Cliff Road

? Nature Center

High Cliff State Park
Observation Tower

General Store
Museum

P
32

HIGH CLIFF
STATE PARK

Red Bird Trail

Lake Winnebago

Lower Cliff Road

Horse/Bike Trail

Old Kiln
Ruins

High Cliff Road

Red Bird Trail

High Cliff Road

Group
Camp Road

Lime Kiln Trail

Indian
Mound Trail

Family Camp Road

High Cliff
State Park
Campground

Horse/Bike Trail

55

HIGH CLIFF
ESCARPMENT
STATE NATURAL AREA

Start this unforgettable hike heading southwest along the top of the escarpment, past the magnificent statue of Chief Red Bird. The first sections of the hike are mostly level, with just a few gentle rollers. You'll score stellar views of the big lake from up here along the escarpment, from overlooks through the stunning forest of maples, elm, and some aspen. The trail passes by an old limestone quarry site and down

Trail through dense forest. DENICE BREAUX

to the Indian mounds area. I always linger a little in places like this, in part to pay silent respect and to soak in the palpable vibe of a fascinating remnant of a people who made their home here upwards of 1,500 years ago.

From the Indian mounds, hang a left and head up a substantial climb past a group of enormous old cottonwoods to the top of the ridge. From here, the Red Bird Trail rolls up and down a series of little valleys back north through the woods to the trailhead.

Miles and Directions

0.0   Hike southwest from the trailhead, along the escarpment.

0.6   Cross the park road.

0.9   At the escarpment natural area and Indian mounds, turn left.

1.2   Pass one trail junction and turn left at the next, heading back north.

1.3   Cross the road again.

2.0   At the junction with the park road, hike along it back to the parking area and trailhead.

2.2   Arrive at the trailhead.

THE GENERAL STORE

Hearken back to the bustling mid-1800s town of High Cliff. The little burg bustled with activity from the lime quarry and in the midst of it all was the General Store. Built from bricks made on-site, the cozy building served as a store, post office, telegraph office, and Western Lime and Cement's office. The store was the quintessential small-town gathering place to meet neighbors, tip a hat to a lady, or just settle into a chair on the porch and watch the goings-on of the day. The building today hosts a museum packed with historical photos and relics from the town's mining heyday.

33 Kohler-Andrae State Park

This popular state park is one of Lake Michigan's last natural preserves, boasting 2 miles of sandy beach, trails through majestic dunes, and rare interdunal wetlands.

Lake or river: Lake Michigan
Photogenic factor: 5
Distance: 1.3-mile linear path; 2.6 miles out and back
Difficulty: Moderate
Hiking time: About 90 minutes
Trail surface: Wooden cordwalk
Other trail users: None

Canine compatibility: Leashed pets allowed north of the nature center only
Land status: State park
Fees and permits: Vehicle pass required
Maps: Park maps; USGS Sheboygan South
Trail contacts: Kohler-Andrae State Park, 1020 Beach Park Ln., Sheboygan 53081; (920) 451-4080; dnr.wi.gov/topic/parks/name/kohlerandrae

Finding the trailhead: From Sheboygan, follow I-43 south to exit 120 (CR V). Follow CR V east 2 miles to its junction with Beach Park Lane and continue straight ahead into the park. Just past the park entrance, turn left and follow Beach Park Lane 0.3 mile to the trailhead. **Trailhead GPS:** N43 67.247' / W87 71.315'

The Hike

Even if you don't hail from the Sheboygan area, you are likely familiar with the Kohler name—if nothing else, simply from standing over a kitchen sink or sitting on a toilet. John Michael Kohler emigrated to the United States in 1854 and worked at his father-in-law's machine shop, later turning it into a household name. Since 1914 the Kohler Company has supplied our country with all manner of plumbing fixtures and today is the nation's second largest in the industry. Mr. Kohler contributed generously to the community, and in return the company donated a large land parcel on the shores of Lake Michigan, which would eventually become John Michael Kohler State Park.

WHAT'S AN INTERDUNAL WETLAND?

Sand dunes are fascinating displays of nature's creativity, and dunes around the Great Lakes take it a step further. Nestled within open dunes or between beach ridges are wetland areas dominated with sedges, rushes, and shrubs, featuring a fluctuating water table in sync with changes in the lake level. Water in these areas warms much faster than the big lakes and provides critical feeding stops for migrating birds and forage for waterfowl like spotted sandpipers, piping plovers, and great blue herons. Dragonflies, midges, damselflies, and many other invertebrates love it here too.

Dune accoutrements. Kent Merhar

Perhaps less known to you is the Terry Andrae name. Mr. Andrae presided over a Milwaukee-based electric company and in 1924 bought 122 acres of lakeshore property. He built a lodge there with his wife and made great efforts to preserve and improve the pine forest and dunes. When Terry died in 1927, his wife Elsbeth donated the land to the state and Terry Andrae State Park was formed.

Additional land was added to the parcels and today both parks are managed as one unit. And what a place it is! The park is packed with a lively array of flora and fauna, from the water to the dunes to the forest. White-tailed deer are common here, of course, as are red foxes, muskrats, and coyotes. More prevalent are at least 150 species of birds living in or visiting the areas. The shoreline is a busy migration corridor in spring and fall and we are treated to raucous crowds of diving ducks, hawks, gulls, warblers, vireos, cranes, and herons. It's a bevy of bird watching!

Not only that, Kohler-Andrae boasts more than 400 plant and 50 tree species, many of which are found only here. And don't miss the Kohler Dunes Natural Area to spot one-of-a-kind dune vegetation and other threatened species.

From the trailhead way at the northern end of the park, hike south on the cordwalk. These ingenious walkways allow up-close access to this fascinating and fragile ecosystem. The trail passes through a small copse of pines and then rolls along and through and over compact meadows filled with a mix of ground-level foliage and short, weather-hardened trees. Some of these dune hollows remind me of enormous golf course sand traps adorned with grasses and shrubbery.

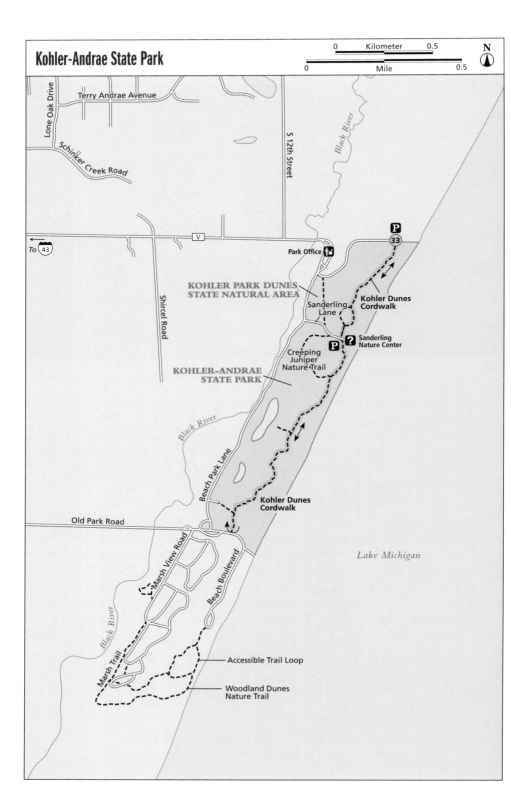

Kohler-Andrae State Park

Kilometer
0   0.5

Mile
0   0.5

N

Lone Oak Drive

Terry Andrae Avenue

Schinker Creek Road

S 12th Street

Black River

V

To 43

Park Office

P
33

KOHLER PARK DUNES
STATE NATURAL AREA

Sanderling
Lane

Kohler Dunes
Cordwalk

Shircel Road

P

Sanderling
Nature Center

Creeping
Juniper
Nature Trail

KOHLER-ANDRAE
STATE PARK

Black River

Beach Park Lane

Kohler Dunes
Cordwalk

Old Park Road

Lake Michigan

Marsh View Road

Beach Boulevard

Black River

Marsh Trail

Accessible Trail Loop

Woodland Dunes
Nature Trail

The scenery escapes worthy superlatives; you'll know what I mean when you hike here. One minute you're ogling faraway views of Lake Michigan's blue expanse and the next you're passing by a soaring sand dune with whiskers of seagrass rustling in the breeze. What a truly special place to be part of, don't you think?

A pair of short spur trails lead to the beach for ample opportunity to mingle with the waves, amble the shoreline, or build a sandcastle. Stop in at the Sanderling Nature Center for intriguing displays and interpretive intel on the dune area, and then continue a winding and rolling course on the cordwalk, passing a few more beach-access trails along the way until arriving at the turnaround point at Old Park Road.

Miles and Directions

0.0 Hike south from the trailhead, following the cordwalk.

0.3 Choose right or left at this junction (both ways meet on the other side).

0.4 Veer left through the nature center parking lot and pick up the trail about halfway down on the lake side.

0.6 Take the left fork, staying on a southerly track.

1.3 The trail ends at Old Park Road. About-face to return to the trailhead.

2.6 Arrive back at the trailhead.

The cordwalk through a meadow. KENT MERHAR

34 Seven Bridges Trail

Don't be surprised if you find yourself hiking this trail with a grin and a spring in your step. It's just plain fun to tap your inner explorer and wander among the trees and cross creeks and hang out on Lake Michigan's sandy shore.

Lake or river: Lake Michigan and 3 unnamed creeks
Photogenic factor: 5
Distance: About a 1.0-mile loop including beach wandering
Difficulty: Easy, with 4 short sections of stairs
Hiking time: About 45 minutes
Trail surface: Hard-packed dirt, with sections of stone

Other trail users: None
Canine compatibility: Leashed pets allowed
Land status: County park
Fees and permits: None
Maps: Park maps; USGS South Milwaukee
Trail contacts: Milwaukee County Parks, 9480 Watertown Rd., Wauwatosa 53226; (414) 257-7275; county.milwaukee.gov

Finding the trailhead: From I-94 in South Milwaukee, exit at College Avenue and head east 4.2 miles to Lake Drive and turn right. Follow Lake Drive south 0.4 mile to Grant Park Drive and turn left. The trailhead is 0.2 mile farther on the left. **Trailhead GPS:** N42 92.311' / W87 84.859'

The Hike

"Enter this wild wood and view the haunts of nature." So says the inscription scrawled into the *Hansel and Gretel*–like wooden archway at the entrance to Grant Park's Seven Bridges Trail, one of Milwaukee's park-system gems.

At nearly 400 acres, Grant Park is the second largest of the string-of-pearls county parks dotting southern Milwaukee's shoreline. In addition to its long-adored hiking trail, Grant Park is home to Milwaukee County's first golf course, established here in 1920 and still a local favorite.

The Seven Bridges Trail was inspired way back in the 1900s by Frederick C. Wulff, the park system's first superintendent of horticulture. Wulff advocated preserving the area's natural state for the enjoyment of the people and developed pathways that would eventually become today's trail system. In the 1930s the Wisconsin Civilian Conservation Corps lent their expertise in developing this area with staircases of slab and wood, as well as lannon stone walkways and, of course, the trademark bridges.

Maybe it's just me, but something happens when I pass under the archway at the trailhead and cross the bridge. Whatever worries happen to be pestering me seem to dissipate and a sense of inward calm takes over. That's a good thing and methinks that will happen with you too.

On the other side of the bridge, the trail delves immediately into a forest thick with maple, beech, yellow birch, ash, and occasional aspen. Among fallen logs draped in moss and along the creek are groundcover species like trout lilies and trillium and other pretty flowers I don't know the names of. Follow the path down through a shallow dip and across a short bridge over the creek. From here it's a flat cruise to the junction with the beach-access trail that descends a short flight of steps and across a bridge to the shore.

And what a treat it is to stroll the sandy beach along the wooded shoreline, skip a rock into the waves, or settle back in a lounge chair and gaze out into Lake Michigan's expanse. The view is nothing short of spectacular, and if you're a fan of glorious sunrises, this is the place to be.

To continue the hike, head back up some stairs and past a junction leading to the park's northern environs. A cool stone bench sits at trail's edge with a great view of the creek below, and then the path comes upon a three-way junction. One direction follows a tributary stream northward and another leads to the Wulff Lodge, where the aforementioned Mr. Wulff once lived with his family. The Seven Bridges Trail follows

Lake Michigan's sandy shore. KENT MERHAR

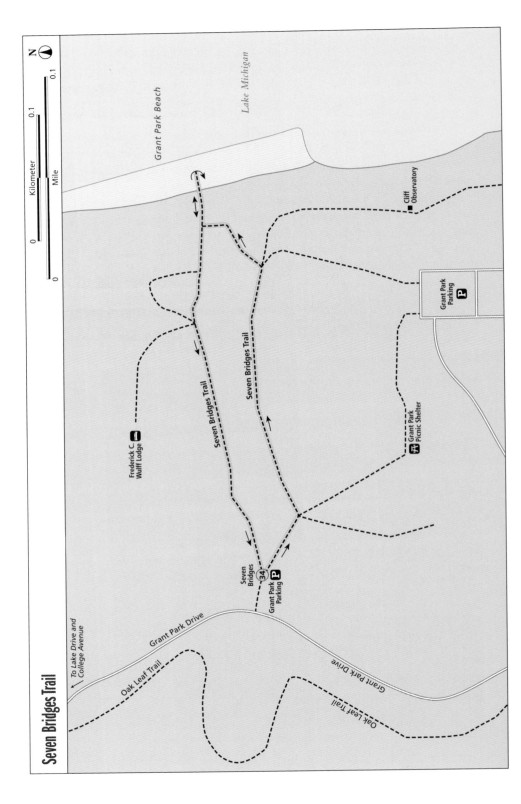

Seven Bridges Trail

Frederick C. Wulff Lodge

Seven Bridges Trail

Seven Bridges Trail

Seven Bridges

34

Grant Park Parking

Grant Park Picnic Shelter

Grant Park Parking

Cliff Observatory

Grant Park Beach

Lake Michigan

Oak Leaf Trail

Grant Park Drive

To Lake Drive and College Avenue

Grant Park Drive

Oak Leaf Trail

N

Kilometer

Mile

0.1

0.1

Classic Lake Michigan. KENT MERHAR

the third option, back toward another creek crossing and the start of a lumpy profile of creeks and bridges and boulders that feels like you're walking right in a *Lord of the Rings* scene.

I found myself lingering more than once along this stretch. I'm a big fan of the sounds of water and this place is chock-full of peaceful vibes. If you stop at the creek and listen, you can hear its stories and its song.

One last bend and crossing of the creek leads to a final flight of steps back to the trailhead. Oh, and one more thing: This part of Grant Park has a reputation of being haunted. Maybe hiking here after dark will be an entirely different experience?

Miles and Directions

0.0   Follow the right fork from the trailhead and descend a short stairway to the first bridge crossing.

0.2   Go left here and follow the path to the beach. Head back the same way to finish the northern section of the loop.

0.4   At the junction with the stairs and trail leading to Wulff Lodge, veer left and cross two more bridges to the final set of stairs back up to the trailhead.

0.6   Arrive back at the trailhead.

35 Milwaukee Lakefront Trail

Milwaukee's lakefront is alive with no end of things to do, from museums to art galleries to unique eateries. This hike follows the Oak Leaf Trail on a loping course through the heart of it all.

Lake or river: Lake Michigan
Photogenic factor: 5
Distance: 3.0-mile lollipop loop
Difficulty: Easy
Hiking time: About 90 minutes
Trail surface: Paved
Other trail users: Bicyclists, runners, skaters

Canine compatibility: Leashed pets allowed
Land status: County park
Fees and permits: None
Maps: Park maps; USGS South Milwaukee
Trail contacts: Milwaukee County Parks, 9480 Watertown Rd., Wauwatosa 53226; (414) 257-7275; county.milwaukee.gov

Finding the trailhead: From I-43, exit at North Avenue and follow it east 2.2 miles to North Terrace Avenue. Turn left and a quick right on East Water Tower Road 0.3 mile to North Lincoln Memorial Drive. Head straight across to the parking area and trailhead. **Trailhead GPS:** N43 05.775' / W87 87.698'

The Hike

In a rare but admirable and much-celebrated effort, the city of Milwaukee long ago chose to underutilize its prized lakefront, sparing it from the ravages of overdevelopment and instead keeping the area natural for all of us to enjoy. Salud!

Laced throughout the metro area is the Oak Leaf Trail, the umbrella name for the city's prized 125-mile trail system, with dozens of trailheads that provide access to most anywhere in the city. The Lakefront Trail segment hugs the Lake Michigan shoreline and takes in the Milwaukee Art Museum, Veterans Park, McKinley Marina, and Bradford Beach at the north end.

The Lakefront Trail stretches from the University of Wisconsin-Milwaukee at the north end to South Milwaukee and includes wildly popular highlights like the

WORLD'S LARGEST MUSIC FESTIVAL

That's a bold claim but Milwaukee's Summerfest backs it up with an official *Guinness Book of World Records* designation. Since 1968 Summerfest has infused the Milwaukee lakefront with eleven days of lively music of nearly every genre from contemporary to gospel to hard rock and reggae. It's a big, big deal, attracting nearly *1 million* people every year. All those fans have plenty to choose from, with more than 1,000 performances taking place on twelve separate stages.

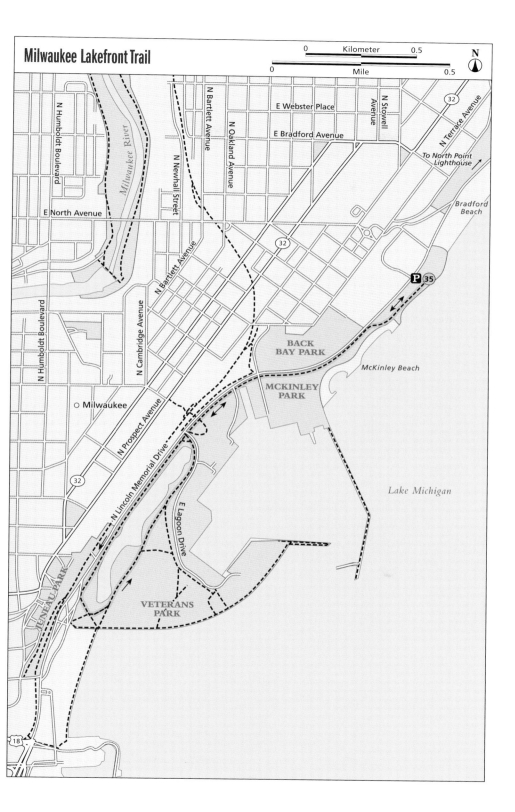

Milwaukee Lakefront Trail

0   Kilometer   0.5

0   Mile   0.5

N

N Humboldt Boulevard

Milwaukee River

N Newhall Street

N Bartlett Avenue

N Oakland Avenue

E Webster Place

N Stowell Avenue

N Terrace Avenue

32

E Bradford Avenue

To North Point Lighthouse

Bradford Beach

E North Avenue

N Bartlett Avenue

32

N Humboldt Boulevard

N Cambridge Avenue

P 35

BACK BAY PARK

o Milwaukee

N Prospect Avenue

MCKINLEY PARK

McKinley Beach

32

N Lincoln Memorial Drive

Lake Michigan

E Lagoon Drive

JUNEAU PARK

VETERANS PARK

18

A quiet space next to the lake. KENT MERHAR

The lakefront's rocky shoreline. KENT MERHAR

Milwaukee Art Museum and the Summerfest grounds. Indeed, this is the place to be in the sunny summer months, where Veterans Park introduces the city to the lake. Here you'll find all kinds of lively events including kite festivals, Brewfest, the Air and Water Show, and lots of great live music.

Looking for a place to stay? Check in at the historically classy Knickerbocker Hotel, and when you're hungry, head to some of the city's choicest dining destinations like Bartolotta's Lake Park Bistro. And don't miss the opportunity to tour Milwaukee's vintage East Side neighborhoods and the impeccably preserved North Point Lighthouse, built in 1888 and one of the city's oldest standing structures.

Start hiking southbound and in short order pass McKinley Beach and its namesake marina. The marina boasts 600 boat slips packed with vessels of all shapes and sizes. Fishing charters ship off from here, or you can take a sailing lesson or rent a Jet Ski to buzz around on the bay.

A bit farther on, the trail reaches Lagoon Drive and skirts the west side of said lagoon down to the Milwaukee Art Museum area. Here you will loop back north through Veterans Park to reconnect with the stem of this hike route for the homestretch back to the trailhead. Conveniently enough, just north of the trailhead is Bradford Beach, the perfect place to unwind after your hike. Kick back in the sand, cool off with a swim, and whatever you do, don't miss a stop at the custard stand for delectable desserts.

Miles and Directions

0.0 From the trailhead, hike south on the Oak Leaf Trail.

0.3 Pass McKinley Beach.

0.8 Cross East Lagoon Drive and the big marina.

1.5 Near the General Douglas MacArthur statue, loop back north on the other side of the lagoon.

2.1 Reconnect with the stem of the trail at East Lagoon Drive.

3.0 Arrive back at the trailhead.

Central Wisconsin and Western Border

Wisconsin's central environs are made of a fascinating blend of rolling hills, transition forest, and wildly diverse ecosystems. Thanks to the back-and-forth sculpting of glaciers, hikes in this region travel along ancient ridgelines and lope from rounded hills to shallow valleys. Moraines and swales, knobs and kettles set the stage, while rare plant species liven the day with color and a who's who of the wildlife crowd wander about. Disappear in a century-old forest on the Straight Lake Trail, visit hilltop lakes along the Chippewa Moraine, and find inspiration among old-growth hemlocks at Brunet Island.

To the west, bucolic Wisconsin countryside of checkerboard farmland unfurls over rolling hills; frisky rivers make lazy curves and oxbows, with accents of riffles and rapids; and the incomparable Coulee Region is our own magic kingdom just waiting

Kinnickinnic State Park. KENT MERHAR

Perrot State Park. KENT MERHAR

to be explored. Options for unforgettable hiking are as wide open and free as a daydream—wander through pioneer history and peer into a 200-foot-deep gorge at Willow River State Park; stroll relaxing trails along the Kinnickinnic and St. Croix Rivers; or go steep in the lumpy bluffs of Perrot State Park.

36 Interstate State Park

Hands down some of the most scenic views in the state. A proud claim perhaps, but one look at the Dalles of the St. Croix and you'll agree this is a very special place.

Lake or river: St. Croix River
Photogenic factor: 5+
Distance: 2.8-mile loop, including a don't-miss 0.4-mile bonus loop
Difficulty: Sections of steep, rocky trail on main loop; easy hiking on short loop
Hiking time: About 90 minutes
Trail surface: Hard-packed dirt with sections of stone and wooden steps and scattered rocks
Other trail users: None

Canine compatibility: Leashed pets allowed
Land status: State park
Fees and permits: Vehicle pass required
Maps: State park maps; USGS Saint Croix Dalles
Trail contacts: Interstate State Park, 1275 State Highway 35, St. Croix Falls 54024; (715) 483-3747; dnr.wi.gov/topic/parks/name/interstate

Finding the trailhead: From WI 35 and US 8, follow WI 35 south 0.5 mile to the park entrance. Take the park road 1.4 miles to the trailhead parking area. Start on the Summit Rock Trail heading north. **Trailhead GPS:** N45 39.446' / W92 64.983'

The Hike

The first time I saw the Dalles of the St. Croix I was sure I'd been transported to Middle-earth. I stood there transfixed. It could've been 5 minutes or 30 and it didn't matter; I was wholly absorbed by the wild, unadulterated, fantasy world magic of the place, and if I wasn't at my desk writing this chapter right now, I'd be back out there.

Foggy forest morning on the St. Croix River. KENT MERHAR

The extraordinary beauty of the Dalles. KENT MERHAR

I have nowhere near enough superlatives (and they would fall far short anyway) to describe to you what the Dalles is all about. It will reach a part of you that perhaps hasn't been reached before, and you will leave inspired by far more than its physical beauty. But in the meantime, give thanks with verve that you are able to be part of something like this if only for a brief moment.

THE ICE AGE TRAIL

It's a 2-billion-year hike back in time on Wisconsin's Ice Age Trail. This stunning National Scenic Trail stretches 1,200 miles from St. Croix Falls in the west to Sturgeon Bay in the east, tracing the outline of the last glacier's terminal moraine 10,000 years ago. Along the way you'll see glacial wonderment in the form of eskers, kames, outwash plains, drumlins, and countless lakes—vivid evidence of how the power of moving ice sculpted our world. More than 600 miles of trail are already marked with yellow blazes, with more added every year. The IAT's phenomenal website is packed with fascinating information and all the latest scoop. Visit www.iceagetrail.org for more information.

Interstate State Park

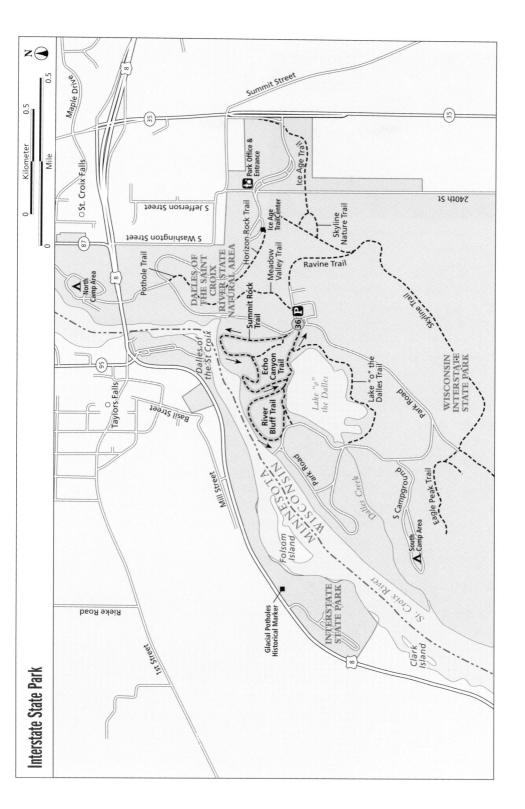

A tributary waterfall above the St. Croix.
KENT MERHAR

If you don't already know this, the Dalles of the St. Croix is a globally rare geologic feature, including the most glacial potholes in an area this size as well as the world's deepest. (I know, that pothole on your town's main street is pretty deep, too, but these have it beat.) Best of all, this part of the river makes up a portion of the St. Croix National Scenic Riverway.

In the 1960s American people finally realized decades of rampant development, water diversion, and logging had imparted untold levels of damage to the surrounding landscapes, its wildlife, and even our drinking water. That awareness inspired Congress to create the National Wild and Scenic Rivers System to preserve the wild nature of our country's most revered waterways. Qualifying for a place in this pantheon of environmental fortitude, a river must first be free-flowing and then provide "remarkably scenic, recreational, geologic, fish and wildlife, historic, cultural, or other similar values."

This riverway is formed by the Namakagon and St. Croix Rivers and flows through 255 miles of some of the upper Midwest's most undeveloped and elegant country. Wetlands, forests, prairies, and the river provide critical habitat for dozens of species of insects, birds, fish, and mammals, some of which are included on threatened and endangered lists.

Start this short and mostly flat hike at the southern Summit Rock Trail parking area and hike north to an overlook of the aforementioned beauteous scenery. Loop back south along the top of the ridge and cliffs to Echo Canyon Trail and trace that path to the River Bluff Trail. This short bonus loop passes by the northern shore of Lake o' the Dalles and then back to the trailhead. **Hot tip:** The Pothole Trail takes in its namesake geology and also includes the life-list overlook I described to start this chapter. Don't miss it.

Miles and Directions

0.0 From the trailhead, follow Summit Rock Trail northbound.

0.5 Follow the trail to the left.

0.75 Turn right on Echo Canyon Trail.

1.4 Turn right on River Bluff Trail. Follow this trail counterclockwise back to the above junction and continue straight to return to the trailhead.

2.8 Arrive at the trailhead.

37 Willow River State Park

This wildly popular state park is packed with variety from open prairie to river gorges, all steeped in pioneer history.

Lake or river: Willow River and Little Falls Lake
Photogenic factor: 4
Distance: 3.4-mile loop
Difficulty: Easy with 1 moderate grade
Hiking time: About 90 minutes
Trail surface: Hard-packed dirt with scattered rocks
Other trail users: None

Canine compatibility: Leashed pets allowed
Land status: State park
Fees and permits: Vehicle pass required
Maps: State park maps; USGS Stillwater, MN
Trail contacts: Willow River State Park, 1034 County Highway A, Hudson 54016; (715) 386-5931; dnr.wi.gov/topic/parks/name/willowriver

Finding the trailhead: From I-94, exit at US 12 and head north 1.6 miles to CR U. Keep going north on CR U for 0.3 mile to its junction with CR A. Follow CR A north 1.5 miles to the park entrance. **Trailhead GPS:** N45 01.736' / W92 67.437'

The Hike

Nearly within shouting distance of Hudson, Willow River State Park is a 3,000-acre playground of prairie, forest, and scenic riverway. The park's namesake river flows in at its northeastern corner, ambles a bit, and roars through a 200-foot gorge before slowing to a crawl at Little Falls Lake, which doubles as a marshy area depending on water flow. From here, the river winds about 3 more crow-fly miles to its confluence with the St. Croix.

As was all the rage in the late 1800s, logging grandly exploited this area, and the Willow River served as a handy transportation corridor to shuttle felled timber to Hudson and lumber mills downstream on the St. Croix. Early settlers also harnessed the river's energy to run four power plants that supplied electricity to Hudson. Three of the four dams have been removed so far, and the area is still in stages of active restoration. Look for evidence of young prairie grasses and wildflowers, plentiful terrestrial wildlife, and all manner of birds, amphibians, and waterfowl.

Prior to logging and settler days, the area's rice lakes were highly coveted by Native American tribes, and 1785's great Battle of Willow River saw the Chippewa and Sioux fighting it out to claim the rice lakes.

Today, this is one of Wisconsin's most visited state parks, with 13 miles of trails, three separate campgrounds, nature center, and, of course, the falls. Rock climbers also flock to the park to take on 5.1 to 5.9 routes on designated walls of the gorge. Winter serves up fun in fifty shades of white, with sledding, snowshoeing, and winter camping.

Heading uphill from the falls. KENT MERHAR

Willow River channels. KENT MERHAR

In warmer months this short hike samples a couple of the park's scenic and historic sections, with close-up views of Willow Falls and its neighboring lake. Head down the hill from the trailhead to the river gorge and take a short side trip to see the

Willow River State Park

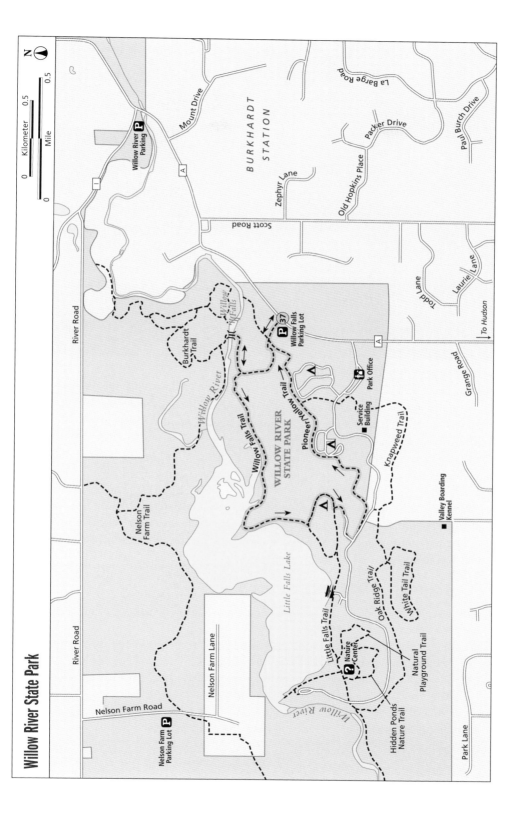

A trail fork beneath puffy clouds. KENT MERHAR

falls. A stairway leads the way along a 100-foot drop in elevation to a close-up view of the lively waterfall. Back on the main route, the heavily wooded trail of maple, aspen, scattered oak, ash, and other species hugs the shoreline of Little Falls Lake, which for much of the year is more of a marsh than a lake. Experts call this an impoundment drawdown; a fancy term for the presence of a dam and associated fluctuations in water level.

From the lake, the trail heads straight for the north side of the 300 Campground. Simply follow the road to the left to meet up with the Yellow Trail. This path squiggles past two more campgrounds and historical grave sites of the area's first white settlers on its way back to the trailhead.

Miles and Directions

0.0 From the Willow Falls parking area, hike past the Yellow Trail and head down a moderately steep grade toward Willow Falls.

0.4 At the trail fork, go right to check out the falls and continue on the main loop on Willow Falls Trail heading west past Little Falls Lake.

2.0 Arrive at the 300 Campground. Turn left and follow the circle road to connect to the Yellow Trail. Follow the Yellow Trail past the 200 Campground and junction with the Orange Trail back to the trailhead.

3.4 Arrive at the trailhead.

38 Straight Lake State Park—Ice Age Trail

This vibrant stretch of the Ice Age Trail takes hikers through unique ecological landscapes packed with rare plant species, diverse wildlife, and a century-old forest.

Lake or river: Straight Lake
Photogenic factor: 4+
Distance: 3.2 miles out and back
Difficulty: Easy
Hiking time: About 2 hours
Trail surface: Hard-packed dirt path
Other trail users: None
Canine compatibility: Leashed pets allowed

Land status: State park
Fees and permits: None required at this trailhead
Maps: State park maps; USGS Luck, WI
Trail contacts: Straight Lake State Park, 2700 120th St., Luck 54853; (715) 431-0274; dnr .wi.gov/topic/parks/name/straightlake/

Finding the trailhead: From Luck, travel east on WI 48 1.8 miles to 140th Street. Turn left and head north 2 miles to 280th Avenue. Turn right. In 0.5 mile the road becomes 130th Street. Continue 0.5 mile to the trailhead parking area. **Trailhead GPS:** N45 61.229' / W92 42.729'

The Hike

Straight Lake is but a baby in Wisconsin's state park system, its land established as such in 2005, but it is the envy of older, more experienced parks. Comprising over 2,000 acres of varied habitats and landscapes, Straight Lake rests in a wonderfully unique area called the Forest Transition Ecological Landscape, a fancy term for a place that supports northern forests as well as agricultural land. This ecological region makes up nearly 7,300 miles and also straddles the Tension Zone, an equally unique area bringing together northern and southern plant and animal species.

And there's more. Within the park is the Tunnel Channel Woods State Natural Area, 457 acres of intact forest with centenarian trees and habitat for many threatened animal species. On the west shore of Straight Lake is the 85-acre Tamarack Fen State Natural Area, another home to rare plants and animals that thrive in its bog, alder, and sedge meadow environment. If you are familiar at all with fens, you know these critical components of nature are rapidly disappearing due to fragmentation, overdevelopment, and other human-caused maladies; anytime we can preserve one is a good day.

As if those accolades weren't enough, Straight Lake State Park is also a Wisconsin Important Bird Area, boasting the likes of trumpeter swans, high numbers of cerulean warblers, yellow-throated vireos, red-shouldered hawks, and bald eagles. The stage is indeed set for an unforgettable hike. From the trailhead, set off into a fairy-tale forest filled with maple, hickory, oak, birch, and pine. The trail soon passes a heartbeat-quiet tamarack fen—mysterious, magical, eerie, and elegant all at once. Places like this

Straight Lake. KENT MERHAR

SAUNTER WITH THOREAU

"It is a great art to saunter." Another of Henry David Thoreau's many inspiring quotes, this one is a core concept of the Ice Age Trail's Saunters Program, a year-round outdoor education program that brings together well over 2,000 students, educators, and community groups around Wisconsin. The program infuses core education programs with a dedication to getting young people outside. The program started in 2008 as a traditional summer school option in Lodi, Wisconsin, and today provides participants with the opportunity to embark on adventures and activities with learning at their core, all while "sauntering" on the trail.

The natural world is an enriching and intoxicating elixir for the mind and soul, and engaging younger age groups with the outdoors has an immediate impact on establishing a healthy lifestyle through a basic, affordable form of exercise. In this program, Saunterers get the benefits of physical activity while improving mental well-being along the way.

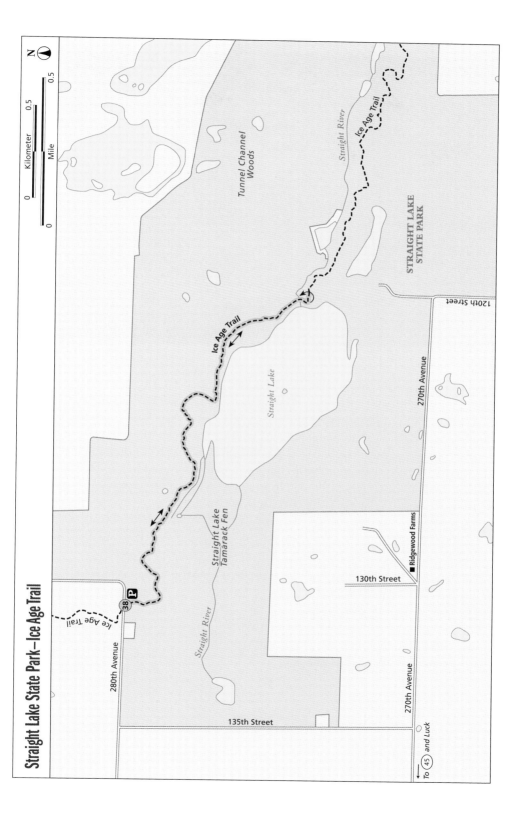

Straight Lake State Park—Ice Age Trail

N

Kilometer
0   0.5

Mile
0   0.5

Ice Age Trail

280th Avenue

P
38

Ice Age Trail

135th Street

Straight River

Straight Lake
Tamarack Fen

Ice Age Trail

Straight Lake

Tunnel Channel
Woods

Straight River

Ice Age Trail

STRAIGHT LAKE
STATE PARK

120th Street

270th Avenue

130th Street

Ridgewood Farms

270th Avenue

To 45 and Luck

Maple forest above Straight Lake. KENT MERHAR

always make me think of misty, shadowy moors. I know I shouldn't go out there but something . . . pulls me . . . closer . . . toward whatever lurks within.

Okay, it's not really that eerie, but for me, Wisconsin's forests have an equally irresistible aura and I have a hard time walking out once I'm there. Nearing the northern shore of Straight Lake, the trail makes a lazy M that takes hikers to intermittent views of the lake through stands of pine. This is a wild and blissfully undeveloped lake and a gradual curve in the trail leads through its peaceful woods to the southeastern corner of the lake, where the Straight River begins its overland journey to Big Round Lake. Enjoy fine water's-edge views from here and follow your tracks back to the trailhead.

Miles and Directions

0.0 From the parking area, hike a couple hundred yards west along the road and dive into the woods on the IAT heading south.

0.4 Pass the tamarack fen to your right.

1.0 The trail hugs close to the northern shore of the lake.

1.6 Turnaround point at the outlet of the Straight River.

3.2 Arrive back at the road and trailhead.

39 Lakefront Park

Feeling like taking an easygoing stroll? Head to Hudson's Lakefront Park for boat-watching and a refreshing, river–borne breeze.

Lake or river: St. Croix River
Photogenic factor: 5
Distance: 1.6 miles out and back
Difficulty: Easy
Hiking time: About 30 minutes
Trail surface: Paved trail
Other trail users: Runners, cyclists

Canine compatibility: Leashed pets allowed
Land status: City park
Fees and permits: None
Maps: City maps; USGS Hudson
Trail contacts: City of Hudson, 505 3rd St., Hudson 54016; (715) 386-0804; www .hudsonwi.gov

Finding the trailhead: From I-94 at the St. Croix River, take the Hudson exit for 2nd Street and follow it north 0.5 mile to Buckeye Street. Turn left and follow Buckeye Street about 1 block to 1st Street and turn right. Parking is available along the park side of the street. **Trailhead GPS:** N44 97.177' / W92 75.857'

The Hike

Downtown Hudson is a blast any time of the year, but like most Wisconsin riverside burgs, it is most alive in the resplendent days of summer. Perhaps nowhere in town is this more evident than Lakefront Park, bustling with activity on shore and off.

If you're a fan of boating, as a skipper or observer, Lakefront is the place to be. You can launch your own skiff from the ramp at the park's south end and pilot it out into the St. Croix River's lively nautical scene, or check out the collection of spiffy vessels at the nearby marina. In the market for a new yacht? St. Croix Yacht Sales is conveniently located close by.

Idyllic views at Lakefront Park.

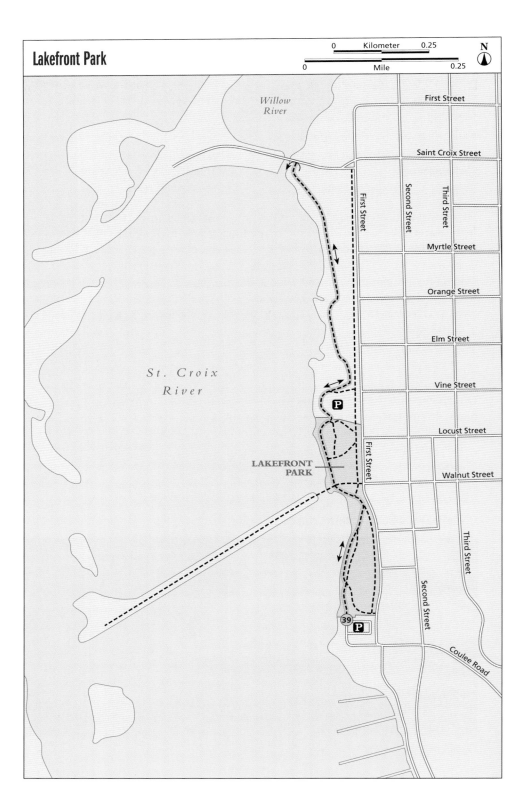

Lakefront Park

Willow River

First Street

Saint Croix Street

First Street

Second Street

Third Street

Myrtle Street

Orange Street

Elm Street

St. Croix River

Vine Street

Locust Street

LAKEFRONT PARK

Walnut Street

First Street

Third Street

Second Street

39 P

Coulee Road

Quiet path along the river.

Speaking of fancy watercraft, for the best boat-watching, walk along the 0.75-mile-long river dike to get a little more up close to the action. Out on the main river channel nearer the Minnesota side, parades of all manner of boats, from inflatable fishing rafts to extravagant yachts, chug along the current, and on weekends it's a veritable waterborne fiesta out there.

Back at the park are picnic shelters, swings and other playground paraphernalia, a pair of sand volleyball courts, swimming beach, and a band shell that hosts a series of summer concerts. It's all great fun and complemented by an upbeat historical downtown area only steps away.

This short hike samples a little of all of it, traveling north from the southern end of the park. A few gentle bends on the paved path lead to the river dike on the water side and archway entrance to downtown on the other. From here the trail passes through a thin stand of trees and past the band shell and arrives at the swimming beach. Jump in if the mood strikes, and then hike on through a mix of woodsy and open areas to the mouth of the Willow River.

About-face here to return to the trailhead.

Miles and Directions

0.0 Set off from the trailhead, hiking north on the paved trail.

0.2 Junction with the river dike.

0.4 Pass the band shell and swimming beach.

0.8 The trail ends at the mouth of the Willow River. Return the same way.

1.6 Arrive back at the trailhead.

THE HISTORIC CASANOVA

In 1896 the Casanova Beverage Company began brewing beer in a 150-foot-deep cave in the hillside just up from the banks of the St. Croix. Prohibition put the brakes on beer making but the company switched gears and bottled soda for Coca-Cola and other companies. Today's restaurant and wine bar hosts an annual beer cave fest where patrons can hang out and quaff brews inside the cave.

40 Chippewa Moraine State Recreation Area–Ice Age Trail

Moraines and swales, knobs and kettles. See it all on this breathlessly scenic hike that winds through gently rolling forest littered with glacial lakes.

Lake or river: North Shattuck Lake
Photogenic factor: 4+
Distance: 1.6 miles out and back; 4.5 miles for entire Circle Trail Loop
Difficulty: Easy
Hiking time: 45–60 minutes, or 2+ hours for full loop
Trail surface: Hard-packed dirt path with scattered rocks

Other trail users: None
Canine compatibility: Leashed pets allowed
Land status: State land
Fees and permits: None
Maps: State park maps; USGS Bloomer
Trail contacts: Chippewa Moraine State Recreation Area, 1339 CR M, New Auburn 54757; (715) 967-2800; dnr.wi.gov/topic/parks/name/chipmoraine/

Finding the trailhead: From Main Street in New Auburn, follow CR SS north to CR M and turn right. Go east on CR M 8 miles to the Chippewa Moraine State Recreation Area entrance road. The trailhead is next to the visitor center. **Trailhead GPS:** N45 13.430' / W91 24.826'

The Hike

Along with drop-dead gorgeous scenery, the Chippewa Moraine area is packed with options. Do a short out-and-back hike to the lakes, make a big loop on the Circle Trail, kick back in a wide-open meadow, or throw on a pack and hit the Ice Age Trail for a multiday adventure. This part of Wisconsin is perforated with dozens of glacially bred lakes tucked in the folds of gently rolling topography and resplendent forests. Distractingly scenic, to be sure, and a great place to connect with your wild side. This is officially called a southern dry mesic forest, and it's packed with colorful and melodious songbirds like scarlet tanagers, cardinals, woodpeckers, and yellow-throated vireos. On the ground you're likely to see white-tailed deer all over the place, and don't be surprised to hear a loud slap on the water from resident beavers.

The Chippewa Moraine region you are walking in today is part of Wisconsin's Ice Age National Scientific Reserve, a group of nine units across the state set aside to protect glacial landscapes with special scientific and scenic value. Established in 1964 as a program of the National Park System, the reserve is loaded with incredible displays of our glacial past for study, outdoor recreation, camping, and birding. Want to learn more? The Chippewa Moraine Chapter of the Ice Age Trail Alliance is your go-to source for all kinds of great events like the Parade of Colors hike and volunteering with trail crews. Find all kinds of great info at www.iceagetrail.org.

Dense hardwood forest on the moraine.

Early fall colors reflect on North Shattuck Lake.

Bridge crossing on the trail.

Tranquil lakeside views from the trail.

Plan some time before or after this hike to check out the well-appointed visitor center, chock-full of fascinating, glacier-inspired information. From the trailhead perched just north of the visitor center, head into the woods on the Ice Age/Circle Trail. The skinny path descends for a short while and makes a buttonhook to the northwest past a little pothole lake. Pass the spur trail to the remote campsite and curve around the northern shore of North Shattuck Lake. By now you've soaked in the outrageous beauty of these woods, and just over a little hill is a perfect spot to stop and enjoy it.

A skinny footbridge passes between North Shattuck and North of North Shattuck Lakes in a magical setting with pines, oaks, and maples on the fringes of these tranquil lakes. A wooden bench conveniently awaits hikers interested in a scenic rest stop. From here it is only a short way around a bend to the south before reaching the junction where the Ice Age Trail heads northwest and the Circle Trail keeps on south. For this hike, simply turn around here to return to the trailhead.

HILLTOP LAKES

The sculpting work of glaciers isn't always about deep gorges and dramatic valleys. In the Wisconsin Glaciation period, depressions in glaciers collected water to form small lakes that were then surrounded by extra-large-sized ice blocks. Assorted debris collected on lake bottoms, and when the ice blocks melted, the debris stayed behind as fine sediment and formed the flat-topped hills we see today. Scoops from the ground attracted meltwater, which in turn created kettle lakes.

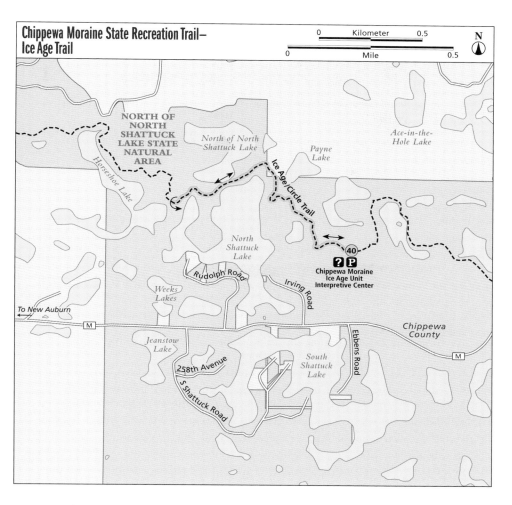

Chippewa Moraine State Recreation Trail–
Ice Age Trail

Hikers completing the Circle Trail Loop will cross CR M and make a long, squiggly curve south and east past kettle lakes and wooded hummocks before looping back to the trailhead.

Miles and Directions

0.0 Follow the Ice Age/Circle Trail left (west) from the trailhead.

0.2 Keep going on the Circle Trail.

0.4 At the junction with the spur trail to a remote campsite, continue around the north end of North Shattuck Lake to a skinny bridge between this and North of North Shattuck Lake.

0.8 At the junction with the Ice Age Trail's divergence to the northwest, turn back here for the short hike or keep heading south to complete the entire Circle Trail.

1.6 Arrive at the trailhead.

41 Brunet Island State Park

Did you know that Cornell University's name was Wisconsin-inspired? This short and scenic hike passes through some of his earliest haunts.

Lake or river: Cornell Flowage
Photogenic factor: 4
Distance: 2.2-mile loop
Difficulty: Easy
Hiking time: About 75 minutes
Trail surface: Hard-packed dirt path
Other trail users: None
Canine compatibility: Leashed pets allowed

Land status: State park
Fees and permits: Vehicle pass required
Maps: State park maps; USGS Cornell
Trail contacts: Brunet Island State Park, 23125 255th St., Cornell 54732; (715) 239-6888; dnr.wi.gov/topic/parks/name/brunetisland

Finding the trailhead: From WI 27 and Bridge Street in Cornell, follow Bridge Street 0.1 mile west to Park Road and turn right. Follow Park Road 1.2 miles to the park entrance. Continue on Park Road to a left turn at 255th Street and follow this road 0.63 mile to the trailhead parking area. **Trailhead GPS:** N45 17.503' / W91 16.920'

The Hike

Born in France in the late 1700s, Jean Brunet eventually found himself in Chippewa Falls, Wisconsin. Brunet built the first dams on the Chippewa River, piloted the first lumber raft to Prairie du Chien and the first steamboat upriver, and was a peacemaker between the Native Americans and white settlers. He also established a trading post at the site of present-day Cornell, oft-visited by Ezra Cornell, the town's future name-sake and key player in the establishment of Cornell University in New York State.

Ezra Cornell was a savvy New York businessman whose land dealings in Wisconsin were instrumental in the university's early years and inspired the naming of the school in his honor. During his land acquisition activity, Cornell often stayed at Jean Brunet's inn and assisted him with timber cruising and related forestry work.

The aura and inspiration of both historical powerhouses is alive on this hike at Brunet Island State Park. Highlighting the hike are giant hemlock trees, remnants of a once-great forest of their ancestors in this area. And these are the last of the biggies. Do you see what is missing on the forest floor? Young hemlocks. Deer are keenly fond of hemlock and overgrazing has put a damper on reestablishing a vibrant tree population. The old will soon pass on; however, forest officials have cordoned off small plots of young hemlock and other native species to help naturally seeded trees establish and grow.

In addition to the maturing trees, you will see club moss, a variety of colorful mushrooms, and wild raspberries and blueberries in more open areas. Keep an eye out

Cornell Flowage from the trail. KENT MERHAR

Bridge crossing along the trail. KENT MERHAR

for foxes, squirrels, porcupine, and grouse in the woods, as well as dozens of songbird species, bald eagles, osprey, and great blue herons. The skies are especially active during spring and fall migrations. Don't miss it!

Start this hike at the picnic area at the island's south tip and trek north on the Timber Trail to the junction with the Pine Trail. Follow this path a short way through stands of its namesake red and white pines to a left turn just before reaching the park road, and head through the woods, cross the road, and walk into the hemlocks on

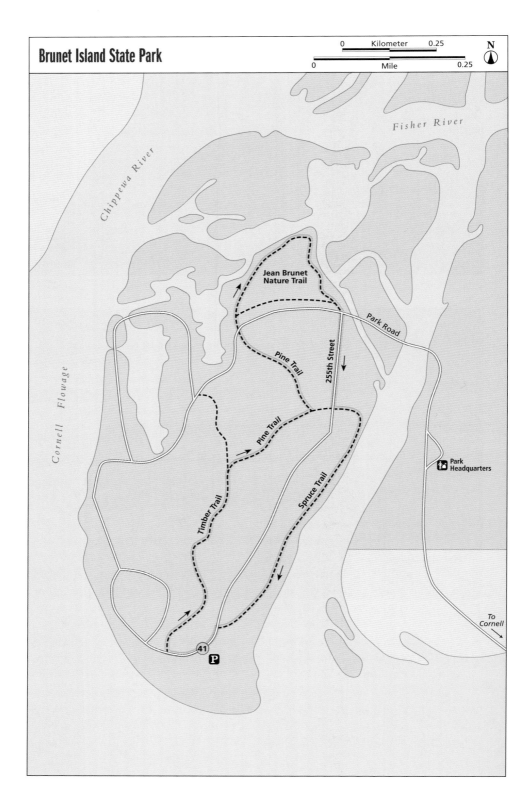

Brunet Island State Park

0   Kilometer   0.25

0   Mile   0.25

N

Fisher River

Chippewa River

Jean Brunet
Nature Trail

Park Road

255th Street

Pine Trail

Cornell Flowage

Pine Trail

Timber Trail

Spruce Trail

Park
Headquarters

41

P

To
Cornell

Peaceful views along the trail. KENT MERHAR

the Jean Brunet Nature Trail. This half-mile jaunt shares space with a few remaining noble hemlocks at the fringe of a Chippewa River backwater.

A short hike on the road connects to the Spruce Trail at the boat landing for the homestretch to the trailhead.

Miles and Directions

0.0   From the trailhead, hike north on the Timber Trail to the junction with the Pine Trail and turn right.

0.8   Pine Trail turns left here.

1.2   Cross the road to the Jean Brunet Nature Trail.

1.6   At the junction with the park road, hike straight ahead along the road.

1.8   At the boat landing, hike on to the Spruce Trail.

2.2   Arrive back at the trailhead.

42 Mondeaux Esker–Aldo Leopold and Ice Age Trails

Walk trails infused with Aldo Leopold's spirit and verve for the natural world. Leopold's land ethic was a driving force in preserving some of our country's most treasured places.

Lake or river: Mondeaux Flowage
Photogenic factor: 5
Distance: 4.4 miles out and back; 1.2 miles on the Leopold Trail
Difficulty: Moderate+ on Mondeaux and easy on Leopold
Hiking time: 2+ hours
Trail surface: Hard-packed dirt path
Other trail users: None

Canine compatibility: Leashed pets allowed
Land status: Chequamegon-Nicolet National Forest
Fees and permits: None required
Maps: Ice Age Trail maps; USGS Mondeaux Dam
Trail contacts: Chequamegon-Nicolet National Forest, 500 Hansen Rd., Rhinelander 54501; (715) 362-1300; fs.usda.gov/cnnf

Finding the trailhead: From North 2nd Street in Medford, follow WI 64 4.5 miles west to CR E. Turn right and head north another 4.5 miles to CR M. Turn left and follow CR M 2 miles to Mondeaux Drive. Go north 8.5 miles to Park Road (FR 1563) and turn right, heading east 1.2 miles to the junction with Campers Road (FR 106) and turn left. Keep following Park Road 0.6 mile to the Mondeaux Dam Recreation Area. The Ice Age Trail skirts the southeastern edge of the parking area.
Trailhead GPS: N45 33.333' / W90 45.187'

The Hike

Eskers and tunnel channels and kettle lakes. It's all part of the day out here on the Mondeaux Flowage segment of the Ice Age Trail. In fact, today's flowage makes part of its home in a 7-mile tunnel channel that at one time roared with glacial meltwater far below the Chippewa Lobe. This area is also loaded with other remnants of glacier handiwork like lake plains flanked with ice-formed walls, cozy kettle lakes, and stubby, rocky knobs covered in dense woods.

A SAND COUNTY ALMANAC

"There are some who can live without wild things, and some who cannot. These essays are the delights and dilemmas of one who cannot."

If you have not yet read Aldo Leopold's conservation epic, do it today. His inspiring essays revealed the workings of the natural world and urged readers to adopt a land ethic that celebrates our true connection with nature. It is a fascinating read and a conservation treasure.

Mondeaux Flowage at the swimming area. KENT MERHAR

Shoreside picnic area. KENT MERHAR

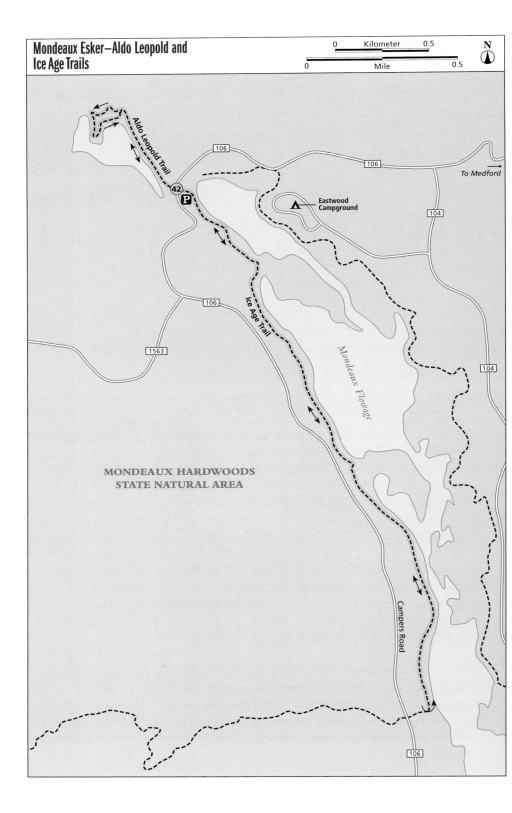

Mondeaux Esker—Aldo Leopold and Ice Age Trails

0   Kilometer   0.5

0   Mile   0.5

N

Aldo Leopold Trail

106

106

To Medford

104

42

P

Eastwood
Campground

Ice Age Trail

106

1563

104

Mondeaux Flowage

MONDEAUX HARDWOODS
STATE NATURAL AREA

Campers Road

106

Reflecting from the Leopold Trail. KENT MERHAR

The ubiquitous hogback ridges around the flowage are also home to glacial eskers, along which part of this trail follows. A huge bonus is the Mondeaux Hardwoods State Natural Area, packed full of all manner of avian life including the very vocal pileated woodpecker, hermit thrush, warblers, scarlet tanager, and many more. Beavers stay true to their busy reputation here, as evidenced by several dammed creeks, and the trail even crosses the tops of longstanding beaver dams.

The Ice Age Trail leaves the parking area at the northern tip of the flowage and follows a short, punchy climb to the top of the esker. Once up top, hikers enjoy stunning forest with occasional views of the flowage through the foliage (say that five times fast). The trail lopes over sometimes-undulating topography and crosses a pair of campground entrance roads, which offer opportunity to shorten your hike should the mood strike, before finally reaching the turnaround at Picnic Point.

Once back to the trailhead, don't miss the Aldo Leopold Trail. This is a great follow-up to the longer hike with a beauty all its own. Rustic and inspiring and enduring just like its namesake, this short path delves into dense, second-growth forest north of the flowage on its way to a most peaceful shoreside setting. At a boot-shaped point, the trail makes a squiggly loop to the waters of a long, skinny lake fed by a glacial spring up near Campers Road. The scenery is nothing short of stupendous, and if you're looking for a quiet, reflective place to rejuvenate your soul, this is it.

However, take heed, fellow hikers: Mosquitoes like it here too. Lots of them. I'm not sure any dosage or hi-test variety of bug spray stands a chance out here in the warm summer months. Be ready or hold off until cooler temps.

Miles and Directions

0.0 Hike south from the trailhead, paralleling the western shoreline of the flowage.

0.4 Cross the entrance road to Spearhead Point Campground.

1.2 Cross the entrance road to West Point Campground.

2.2 Arrive at Picnic Point Campground. Turn around here for the return trip.

4.4 Arrive back at the trailhead.

43 Kinnickinnic State Park

The "Kinni" is revered by Wisconsinites for its outstanding fishing and solitudinous factor. This leisurely hike wanders through some of the park's scenic standouts, with a side trip down the bluff to the St. Croix.

Lake or river: St. Croix River
Photogenic factor: 4+
Distance: 2.6-mile loop, with option for over 5 additional miles
Difficulty: Easy with 1 steep section to the river
Hiking time: About 1 hour
Trail surface: Hard-packed dirt and gravel and short paved section
Other trail users: None

Canine compatibility: Leashed pets allowed
Land status: State park
Fees and permits: Vehicle pass required
Maps: State park maps; USGS Prescott
Trail contacts: Kinnickinnic State Park, W11983 820th Ave., River Falls 54022; (715) 425-1129; dnr.wi.gov/topic/parks/name/kinnickinnic/

Finding the trailhead: From I-94 in Hudson, exit at CR F and head south 9 miles to 820th Avenue. Turn right and the park entrance is 0.2 mile on the left. Follow the park road 1.2 miles to the picnic and trail parking area on the left. **Trailhead GPS:** N44 83.401' / W92 75.139'

The Hike

It looks like a tranquil, meandering stream, and while it is indeed a beauty, the Kinni is a DNR-designated Outstanding Resource Water and nationally recognized Class I trout stream boasting stretches of more than *8,000* trout per mile. This gorgeous, spring-fed river runs 22 miles through idyllic western Wisconsin countryside, with a 174-square-mile watershed that includes 40 percent of the state's plant species, 50 percent of bird species, and nearly fifty types of critters on the endangered, threatened, or special concern list.

Admirable qualities, to be sure, and we're proud to call the Kinni our own. This short hike starts in the heart of the park on the Orange Trail, skirting the edge of a prairie for a few dozen steps before it heads into dense woods of largely mixed hardwood, with red and white pine scattered about. A half mile later the path meets the junction with the Purple Trail. Follow this trail as it curves along the top of the river gorge, with intermittent views to the river below.

ANCIENT ORIGINS

Fun-to-say Kinnickinnic (originally spelled with a k at the end) is an early Native American smoking mixture made from a combination of plant leaves and various barks. In fact, the Ojibwa meaning is literally "things that are mixed."

Great views of the St. Croix from the park bluffs. KENT MERHAR

Short paved trail to the river. KENT MERHAR

When the trail reaches the picnic area at the far western end of the park, linger for a bit at the overlook above the Kinnickinnic Delta far below, then take the short, steep paved path down to the swimming beach and outrageous upstream views of the

Kinnickinnic State Park

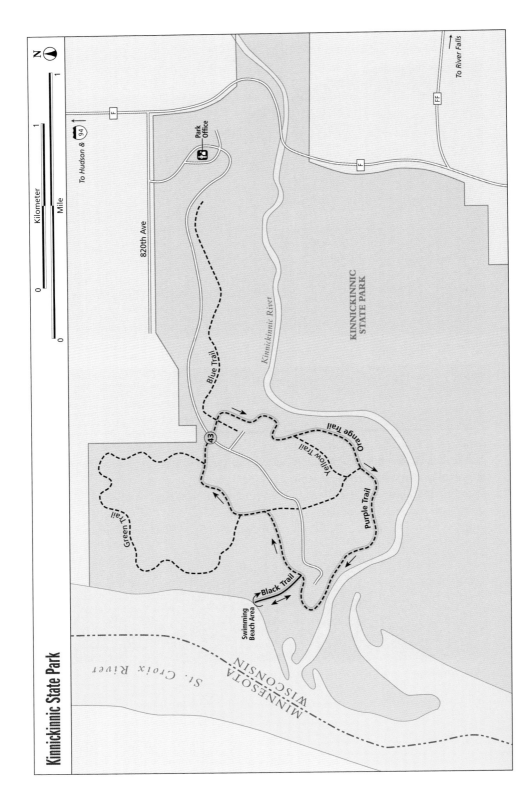

St. Croix River. The Kinni empties into the St. Croix through the trees just south of here, and on sunny summer weekends, the St. Croix bustles with water-based activity when vessels of all shapes and sizes take to the water like ants to a picnic basket. Even if you don't have a picnic basket, it's fun to kick back and watch all the boats float up and down the river.

After a break, head back uphill and hop back on the Purple Trail. In short order you'll meet the Yellow Trail and turn left, passing an optional 1-mile loop on the Green Trail. The main loop crosses the park road and leads right back to the parking area and trailhead. *Insider tip:* Don't miss plunging down the sledding hill in winter and snowshoeing through the woods along the gorge.

Miles and Directions

0.0 Set off from the trailhead on the Orange Trail, past the prairie and into the trees.

0.4 At the junction with the Purple Trail, turn left.

1.1 Arrive at the picnic area and overlook. Head 600 feet downhill to the river and back up to continue on the Purple Trail.

1.6 At the junction with the Yellow Trail, turn left.

2.6 Arrive at the trailhead.

A peaceful vibe at riverside. KENT MERHAR

44 Perrot State Park

This lumpy park in Wisconsin's southwest is home to the confluence of the Trempealeau and Mississippi Rivers and sublime views of the valley from Perrot Ridge or Brady's Bluff.

Lake or river: Mississippi River
Photogenic factor: 4+
Distance: 3.1-mile loop
Difficulty: Moderate with 2 steep climbs (many other trail options available)
Hiking time: 2+ hours
Trail surface: Hard-packed dirt with scattered roots and rocks, and a section of stairs

Other trail users: None
Canine compatibility: Leashed pets allowed
Land status: State park
Fees and permits: Vehicle pass required
Maps: State park maps; USGS Winona, MN
Trail contacts: Perrot State Park, W26247 Sullivan Rd., Trempealeau 54661; (608) 534-6409; dnr.wi.gov/topic/parks/name/perrot

Finding the trailhead: From La Crosse, follow US 53/WI 35 north 9.7 miles to the WI 35 exit. Head west 7.7 miles to Main Street in Trempealeau. Turn left and go 3 blocks to 1st Street. Turn right and follow this road (which becomes South Park Road) 1.9 miles to the park entrance. **Trailhead GPS:** N44 01.626' / W91 47.542'

The Hike

Think back 500 million years or so when an enormous inland sea covered today's Wisconsin. All that water drained as the land rose, and later another sea moved in. The advance and retreat of these inland seas piled up lots of mud and debris, creating the dramatic sandstone bluffs of today's Perrot State Park. Many of these steep, lumpy bluffs rise to more than 500 feet above verdant wetlands, open fields, and deep valleys; providing homes to hundreds of species of flora and fauna.

Indeed, Perrot is a veritable who's who of the upper Midwest nature scene, including water-loving critters like beavers, mink, waterfowl, various turtles, all sorts of frogs and toads, and muskrats. Dense forests harbor plentiful white-tailed deer, foxes, woodchucks, and squirrels. But perhaps the park's most popular wildlife highlight is

WISCONSIN'S DRIFTLESS AREA

The last glacier that slunk down slowly from present-day Canada is responsible for much of Wisconsin's varied landscapes—*except* for the southwestern corner. The conglomeration of silt, sand, boulders, and other assorted debris left in the wake of glaciers is called drift. The giant glacier skipped this part of the state, hence its Driftless Area name, leaving behind outrageously beautiful forested bluffs, deep coulees, and bucolic valleys.

The Mississippi River valley from Perrot Ridge. KENT MERHAR

Trempealeau Mountain at sunset. KENT MERHAR

A long climb to the top. KENT MERHAR

The Mississippi River. KENT MERHAR

found overhead. Well over 200 species of birds live in or migrate through this area every year, including warblers, fly-catchers, vireos, and untold numbers of eagles and hawks. You might even catch a glimpse of tundra swans in the spring.

In addition, the park includes two Wisconsin State Natural Areas: Brady's Bluff Prairie and Trempealeau Mountain. Brady's is a dolomite-capped bluff bursting with native Wisconsin plants like needle grass, prairie larkspur, and silky aster. Several rare butterfly species live here too. Across the Trempealeau River stands its namesake mountain at 425 feet and covered in oak, basswood, and maple. A long time ago the mountain served as a handy navigational reference for river travelers and merchants and also hosts many Native American burial sites and other evidence of the area's rich history. Hikers can score stellar views of this hill from the top of Brady's.

About a dozen steps from the West Brady's Trailhead, the ground points upward in a hurry. Keep chugging along and near last pitch before the summit, a very long set of stairs clings to the rocks to aid your final, heroic push. Okay, so it's not as dramatic as Everest and a tad lower in elevation, but the views from the top of Brady's take your breath away all the same. Trempealeau Mountain is front and center in the foreground to the north, along with ridiculously gorgeous views of bluffs on the Minnesota side and the long, winding upstream ribbon of the Mississippi. Views south are equally sublime and after soaking it all in, head off northeast and drop down from the bluff into the shallow saddle between Brady's and Perrot Ridge.

By now you've likely noticed the colorful and lively display of resident woodland flowers in the form of Dutchman's breeches; phlox; violets in blue, yellow, and white; ferns; and bellworts. Especially in spring, the park is chock-full of aromatic plants dressed to the nines.

Follow the Perrot Ridge Trail south, round the bulbous southern nose of the ridge, and hoof it up a short, steepish climb to the top for more life-list views. Descend and connect with the downhill trail to the park office and East Brady's Trailhead. Find the Riverview Trail at the edge of the parking area and wander this flat stretch along the railroad tracks and river back to the West Brady's Trailhead.

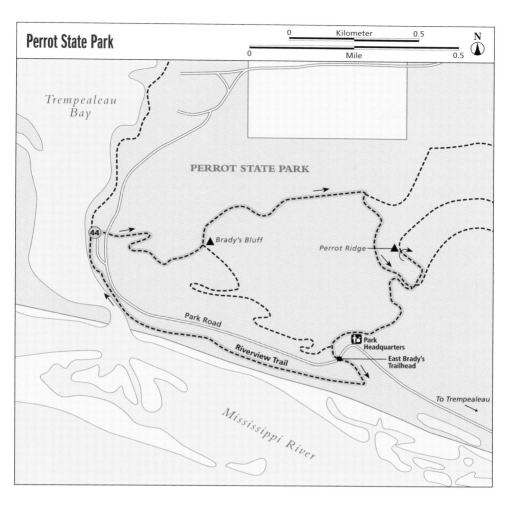

Perrot State Park

Trempealeau Bay

PERROT STATE PARK

Brady's Bluff

Perrot Ridge

Park Road

Riverview Trail

Park Headquarters

East Brady's Trailhead

To Trempealeau

Mississippi River

Miles and Directions

0.0 From the West Brady's Trailhead, head into the woods, rapidly gaining elevation.

0.4 Reach the summit of Brady's Bluff and junction with the East Brady's Trail. Turn left.

0.9 At the junction with the Perrot Ridge Trail, turn right.

1.3 Pass this junction but remember it as you'll return here for the descent. Continue to the left to reach the short climb to Perrot Ridge.

1.4 Turn left here for a short climb to the top of Perrot Ridge. Ogle the views and return to the junction you passed earlier.

1.9 Go left here for the descent to the East Brady's Trailhead.

2.2 Arrive at the East Brady's Trailhead. Head for the southeast corner and follow the sign for the Riverview Trail.

3.1 Arrive at West Brady's Trailhead.

45 Wyalusing State Park

Score bluff-top views of two rivers, some of the state's best bird watching, and explore the Treasure Cave on this long loop in Wisconsin's far southwest.

Lake or river: Mississippi and Wisconsin Rivers
Photogenic factor: 4+
Distance: 4.1-mile loop
Difficulty: Moderate
Hiking time: 2+ hours
Trail surface: Hard-packed dirt path
Other trail users: None
Canine compatibility: Leashed pets allowed

Land status: State park
Fees and permits: Vehicle pass required
Maps: State park maps; USGS Brodtville, and USGS Clayton, IA
Trail contacts: Wyalusing State Park, 13081 State Park Ln., Bagley 53801; (608) 996-2261; dnr.wi.gov/topic/parks/name/wyalusing

Finding the trailhead: From the junction of US 18 and WI 35 at the south end of Prairie du Chien, follow US 18 south 5 miles to CR C and turn right. Follow CR C south 3.1 miles to CR X and turn right. Go 1 mile west to the park entrance. Follow the park road 2 miles to the Green Cloud Picnic Area. The hike starts adjacent to the picnic shelter. **Trailhead GPS:** N42 98.869' / W91 12.869'

The Hike

In the nineteenth century Munsee-Delaware Native American tribes settled in this area at the confluence of the Mississippi and Wisconsin Rivers. In their Lenape language, *Wyalusing* means "home of the warrior." One can imagine proud tribes defending this special place of 500-foot-high bluffs and dense forests above the rivers. Indeed, effigy-shaped burial mounds dating back 3,000 years are evidence this area was held sacred for generations.

Today, Wyalusing State Park is 2,700 acres of dramatic bluff-top views, caves and fissures, and fantastic rock formations, along with wetlands, a canoe trail, river backwaters, and waterfalls. In the midst of it all is a long list of celebrity wildlife from the water to high overhead. Be on the lookout for beavers, foxes, deer, bald eagles, turkey vultures, and several other raptor species.

Nearly one hundred bird species live here, with many more migrating through in spring and fall. You see and hear colorful songbirds, great horned owls, and woodpeckers of various ilk. At ground level, look for wild turkey, white-tailed deer, snakes, squirrels, and lots more. The wetlands and river are home to all manner of waterfowl like herons, egrets, muskrats, minks, beavers, and wood ducks.

This revered state park, originally named Nelson Dewey, is more than one hundred years old, and its present form hosts two popular campgrounds, naturalist programs, and a host of other activities such as bicycling, fishing and hunting, and cross-country skiing in winter. The park also holds national status through the

Epic river valley views. Dixie Brumm/WI DNR

Wyalusing Hardwood Forest, a National Natural Landmark; and the Wyalusing State Park Mounds Archeological District. Throw in the Wyalusing Hardwood Forest SNA and you've got yourself a packed lineup of nature's best stuff.

One of the highlights for hikers of course is ogling sprawling panoramic views, of which there are many, and you get a couple dandies on this gem of a hike. Head north from the Green Cloud Picnic Area to the junction with the Old Immigrant Trail, which descends the bluff via a few switchbacks to the river, where a bench awaits for a relaxing midhike break. From here, the path makes a sweeping curve through the woods on its climb back up the bluff and the junction with the Bluff Trail. Follow

SENTINEL RIDGE

At Wyalusing State Park's western boundary, Sentinel Ridge rises high above the Mississippi River Valley. On this ridge, 69 of more than 130 Indian burial mounds are carefully preserved. Many original mounds were destroyed by rampant stone quarrying or farming, but we are fortunate today to share this space with the remaining mounds. The Sentinel Hill and Procession mound groups are made of twenty-eight mounds in linear formation following the crest of the bluff. Archaeologists and historians believe at least two separate periods of mound building were present in this area, with evidence including stone crypts, copper celt, and stone pipe.

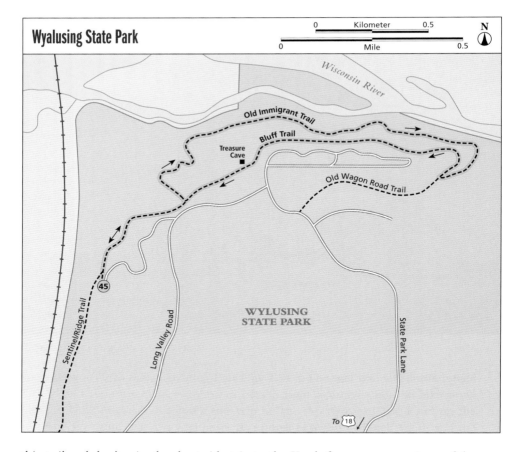

this trail and don't miss the short side trip to the Knob for outrageous views of the Wisconsin River.

Keep on truckin' on the Bluff Trail and soon arrive at the short trail to Treasure Cave, one of the park's go-to destinations. A steep staircase leads up to the cave, and inside, you can shinny along through a narrow passage to a hidden chamber. Very cool stuff. Back on the trail are a couple more stairways, a stone archway, and another pair of overlooks.

At the Old Immigrant junction, simply follow the Sentinel path back to the trailhead.

Miles and Directions

0.0 From the trailhead, hike north on the Sentinel/Ridge Trail.

0.3 At the junction with the Old Immigrant Trail, turn left.

2.9 At the junction with the Bluff Trail, turn right.

3.8 At the junction with the Sentinel/Ridge Trail, keep going straight ahead.

4.1 Arrive back at the trailhead.

Southern Reaches

I n Wisconsin's far south, hikers are treated to a little bit of everything, from steep bluffs and postcard scenery at Devil's Lake State Park to off-the-grid forest to relaxing lakeside walks at UW's Arboretum and adjacent reserve. Whatever your fancy, you'll find it here, and your hiking boots will thank you.

Looking for insider tips from the author? Put Gibraltar Rock on your list right now and go there soon. You get a fun climb up the big rock and views of the Wisconsin River Valley are outrageously gorgeous. Devil's Lake is nothing short of magical and packed with frame-worthy views. In the Glacial Plains regions near Madison, check out Pheasant Branch Conservancy for quiet, streamside walks and panoramic views; or wander among wildflowers and wildlife at Governor Dodge State Park.

Lakeshore Nature Preserve. DENICE BREAUX

46 Chapel Gorge Trail–Dells of the Wisconsin River SNA

Escape the Wisconsin Dells tourist circus on this short hike into a 500-million-year-old fairy-tale gorge, complete with a sandy beach and bucket-list photo ops.

Lake or river: Wisconsin River
Photogenic factor: 4+
Distance: 1.8-mile lollipop loop
Difficulty: Easy with 1 steep descent and ascent at the river gorge
Hiking time: About 45 minutes
Trail surface: Hard-packed dirt with a section of steps
Other trail users: None

Canine compatibility: Leashed pets allowed
Land status: State land
Fees and permits: None
Maps: Map in this book; USGS Wisconsin Dells North
Trail contacts: Wisconsin Department of Natural Resources, 101 S. Webster St., Madison 53707; (888) 936-7463; dnr.wi.gov

Finding the trailhead: From I-90/94, exit at WI 13 for Wisconsin Dells and follow the highway 1.4 miles across the Wisconsin River to River Road. Turn left and follow River Road 1.7 miles north to the SNA parking area on the left. The trail starts at the north end of the lot. **Trailhead GPS:** N43 64.874' / W89 77.504'

The Hike

This is the tale of two Dells. There's the town of Wisconsin Dells, the water park capital of the world, with theme parks, endless lineups of RVs, water slides, and mini-golf. And there's the real Dells of the Wisconsin River, a spectacular treasure of calendar-worthy scenery and globally rare plant species.

More than 5 miles of rugged river corridor make up one of the state's most photogenic and scientifically significant locations. The deep gorge, over 100 feet deep in places, is creased with tributary canyons and 500-million-year-old rock formations carved by water and wind. Cracks and crevasses in the cliffs hold moisture and provide microenvironments for plants, one of which is the cliff cudweed, a tiny aster that grows only here and on protected rock ledges in the Kickapoo Valley southeast of La Crosse—nowhere else on Earth. Other rare plants found here include the Lapland azalea, fragrant fern, and maidenhair spleenwort.

Rare animal life is also present in the area, including six mussel species, six dragonfly species, and a number of different birds. Much archaeological evidence has also been found here, dating back through thousands of years of Native American peoples. Visitors and scientists have discovered burial mounds, effigy mounds, and many camp and village sites.

Aged stone steps ascend from the beach.
KENT MERHAR

Wide trail through the woods.
KENT MERHAR

Up close with the Wisconsin River. KENT MERHAR

Chapel Gorge Trail—Dells of the Wisconsin SNA

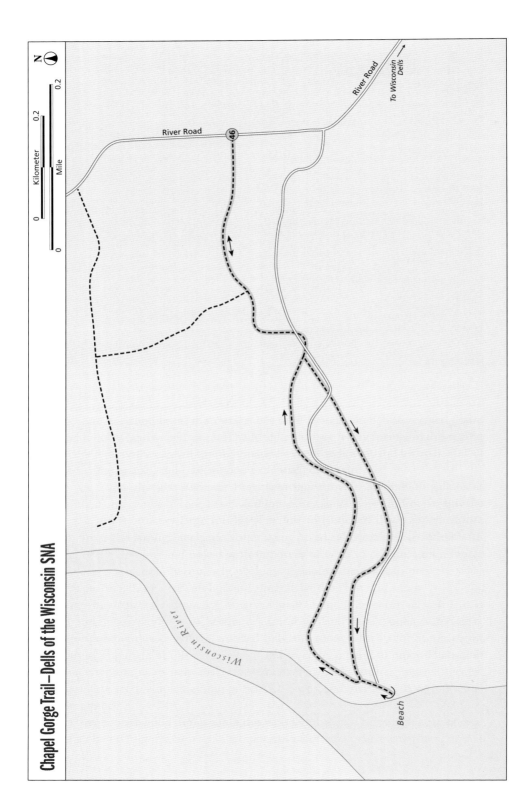

N

Kilometer
0   0.2   0.2

Mile
0   0.2

River Road

46

River Road

To Wisconsin
Dells

Wisconsin River

Beach

THE ART OF GLACIERS

Think back 19,000 years or so when the present-day Dells area was within sight of the far western fringe of an enormous continental glacier. As the glacier melted, it formed the sprawling and deep Glacial Lake Wisconsin, held in lake form by a huge ice dam left over from the glacier. The dam eventually burst, causing a devastating flood that cut the deep, narrow gorges and fantasy-world rock formations we see today.

Even the uplands above the gorge support a wide range of ecosystems like oak savanna, dry oak forest, and northern mesic forest of hemlock, oak, and pine.

Primed with excitement to delve into this fascinating world, hike west from the trailhead through hardwood forest, pass under a giant power line, and then proceed back into the woods. Go left at the trail split, and in a short while the trail descends steeply along the cliff to small and secluded Birchcliff Beach, which is essentially a river sandbar. This is a very popular summer destination for crowds of boats and wanderlust souls, so don't be surprised to see lively scenes hereabouts.

However, you will also have great views of the high sandstone cliffs upstream where the river cuts through the Narrows. When you're ready, hike to the northern end of the beach to the trail heading back into the woods and up to the top of the cliff. Here the path leads back east. At the junction turn left and follow the last stretch back to the trailhead.

Miles and Directions

0.0 From the trailhead, hike through woods of mixed hardwood sprinkled with Norway pine.

0.4 At the split, go left.

0.6 Arrive at the beach. Plan to linger, then hike back up the ridge via the trail at the northern end of the beach to return via the northern leg of the loop.

1.8 Arrive back at the trailhead.

47 Wisconsin Dells Scenic Riverwalk

This short riverside gem is a relaxing intermission from the tourist circus. Bonus points for postcard sunsets and a tasty beverage at the Riverwalk Pub.

Lake or river: Wisconsin River
Photogenic factor: 4+
Distance: 1.0 mile out and back
Difficulty: Easy
Hiking time: 30–45 minutes
Trail surface: Paved
Other trail users: Runners, bicyclists
Canine compatibility: Leashed pets allowed

Land status: City of Wisconsin Dells
Fees and permits: None
Maps: Various city maps; USGS Wisconsin Dells North
Trail contacts: Wisconsin Dells Visitor and Convention Bureau, 701 Superior St., Wisconsin Dells 53965; (800) 223-3557; wisdells.com

Finding the trailhead: The trail starts at the west end of the parking lot in the Dells arts district at Broadway Avenue and River Road. **Trailhead GPS:** N43 62.781' / W89 77.690'

The Hike

Thanks to foresight from the mayor's office and local business owners, Wisconsin Dells extended its prized Riverwalk to a half mile in 2016, offering visitors can't-miss river gorge views, interpretive stations, and overlooks. Got an urge to play checkers? A games table and comfy benches are strategically located along the path for welcome (and free) respite from the din of water slides, zip lines, and mini-golf. Top it off with a cold brew and beauteous views from the patio at the Riverwalk Pub and you've got yourself the makings of a splendid afternoon.

From Broadway Avenue, the trail curves to an overlook of the boat-tour dock, the railroad trestle bridge, and the topside of Kilbourn Dam. A barely there descent leads from here into shady woods and then past the pub. There's an overlook up ahead next to River Road with outrageously beautiful views upstream and down. By happenstance I strolled past here at the colorful crescendo of a heavenly sunset made of all manner of pinks and purples. Bring your camera.

THE WATER PARK CAPITAL OF THE WORLD

If you or the kids are in the mood for lively distraction after quiet hiking in the woods, this is the place. Wisconsin Dells holds title as the Water Park Capital of the World, with all manner of moving liquid delight and ancillary activities such as zip lines, mini-golf, heated pools, and live entertainment. Visitors can also find casinos, golf courses, amusement parks, museums, and spas.

Elevated Wisconsin River views. KENT MERHAR

The Riverwalk and neighboring gazebo. KENT MERHAR

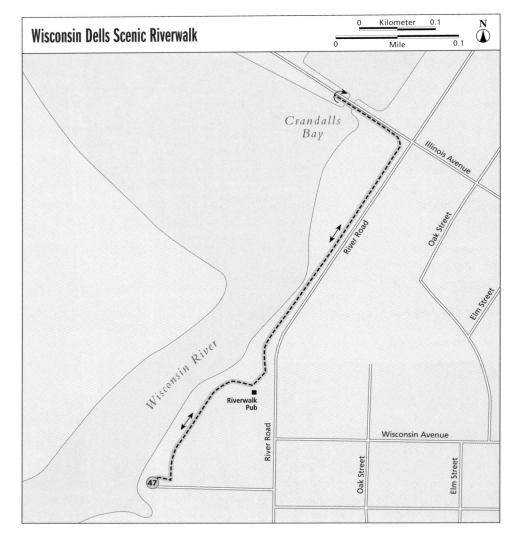

Wisconsin Dells Scenic Riverwalk

0 Kilometer 0.1

0 Mile 0.1

N

Crandalls Bay

Illinois Avenue

Oak Street

Elm Street

River Road

Wisconsin River

■
Riverwalk
Pub

Wisconsin Avenue

Oak Street

Elm Street

River Road

47

Past the overlook, the trail crosses the River Road bridge and makes a hard left at Illinois Avenue before ending on the north side of the bridge above Crandalls Bay. Stay tuned—plans are in the works to continue the Riverwalk farther north.

Miles and Directions

0.0 From the trailhead, check out the first overlook of the dock and dam and then pass through a woodsy area.

0.1 Pass the Riverwalk Pub.

0.2 Ogle the views from the River Road overlook.

0.5 At the trail terminus at Crandalls Bay, retrace your tracks back to the trailhead.

1.0 Arrive at the trailhead.

48 Echo-Lakeview Loop—Mirror Lake State Park

Packed with hiking options, Mirror Lake State Park gives you the chance to go slow and easy, mingle with the rest of the visitors, or trek to quieter environs.

Lake or river: Mirror Lake
Photogenic factor: 4
Distance: 3.8-mile loop
Difficulty: Easy to moderate
Hiking time: About 2 hours
Trail surface: Hard-packed dirt path with a paved section on Echo Rock Loop
Other trail users: None
Canine compatibility: Leashed pets allowed

Land status: State park
Fees and permits: Vehicle pass required
Maps: State park maps; USGS Wisconsin Dells South
Trail contacts: Mirror Lake State Park, E. 10320 Fern Dell Rd., Baraboo 53913; (608) 254-2333; dnr.wi.gov/topic/parks/name/mirrorlake/

Finding the trailhead: From I-90/94, exit at US 12 and head south 0.4 mile to Moon Road. Turn right and head west 0.2 mile to Fern Dell Road. Follow Fern Dell west 1.2 miles to the park entrance. Follow the park road all the way to its end at the Echo Rock Trailhead.
Trailhead GPS: N43 57.204' / W89 80.820'

The Hike

We've seen the name *dells* in several chapters of this book and here it is again. In French, *dalles* means gorge, and Wisconsin has lots of them. Just south of the hubbub of Wisconsin Dells are more *dalles*; this time at Mirror Lake State Park, courtesy of Dell Creek.

Here's what geologists believe: When the colossal Wisconsin Glacier covered most of Wisconsin upwards of 20,000 years ago, its western reaches ended near the present-day park. Dell Creek lies wholly in our state's non-glaciated regions, but theory has it that glacial outwash dammed and diverted the creek where it merrily carved the channel now containing Mirror Lake. Pretty cool, huh?

Not only that, but these photogenic gorges are made of 500-million-year-old sandstone deposited here via rivers draining from inland seas. When the seas finally retreated, the sand compacted into today's geologic wonders.

Flora and fauna are big hits here as well. Mirror Lake itself is surrounded by pine and oak woods and wildflower-filled prairies. In fact, the Mirror Lake Pine Oak Forest, at the park's northwest corner, is one of Wisconsin's State Natural Areas. This SNA is loaded with a fascinating display of white pine and oak scattered around sandstone cliffs and vernal ponds. The gently undulating topography is littered with

Smooth trail through the forest. KENT MERHAR

showy shrubs like low blueberry, swamp dewberry, and wintergreen. At ground level look for wild sarsaparilla, jack-in-the-pulpit, and enchanter's nightshade.

In the midst of it all live critters such as deer, squirrels, chipmunks, muskrats, rabbits, and coyotes. Above you can see pileated woodpeckers, barred owl, various raptor species, pine warblers, and many other songbird species.

Start this hike out with some of the park's best scenery on the short Echo Rock Trail. Loop past a skinny section of Mirror Lake and wander down steps and among boulders, and then angle toward the Lakeview Trail. This path parallels the shoreline on its way past the Sandstone Ridge Campground and various picnic and playground areas. Keep the same course all the way, following the lumpy terrain to the end of the long, narrow bay and the western trail cluster.

You will instantly notice the difference in decibels as you leave the buzz of the campgrounds and nearby interstate behind. Follow the Northwest Trail in that direction, through stands of Scotch and white pine mixed with big ol' white oaks, cherry, and maple, to the tip of the peninsula and the junction with Wildwood Pass Trail. This will take you back south to the start of these trails, where you simply follow the Lakeview Trail back to the trailhead.

Mirror Lake view from the trail. Kent Merhar

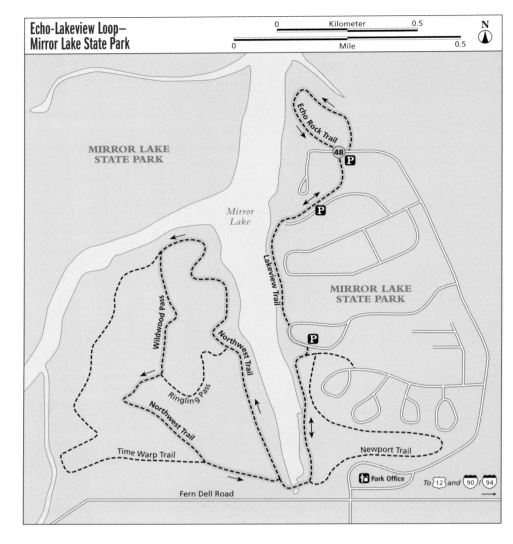

0   Kilometer   0.5   N

0   Mile   0.5

MIRROR LAKE
STATE PARK

Echo Rock Trail

48

P

P

Mirror
Lake

Lakeview Trail

MIRROR LAKE
STATE PARK

P

Wildwood Pass

Northwest Trail

Ringling Pass

Northwest Trail

Time Warp Trail

Newport Trail

Park Office

To 12 and 90 / 94

Fern Dell Road

Miles and Directions

0.0 From the trailhead, hike the Echo Rock Trail counterclockwise. Back at the trailhead junction, continue south through the parking area and connect with the Lakeview Trail. Follow this south to the loop road parking areas and connect with the western stretch of the Newport Trail to its junction with the nature trail and Purple Trail cluster.

0.8 At the junction with the Purple Trails, take an immediate right and follow the Northwest Trail.

2.0 At the junction with the Wildwood Pass Trail, turn left.

2.6 Turn left and follow the Purple Trail back to the Newport Trail junction. Turn left at Newport and follow the same route back to the trailhead.

3.8 Arrive back at the trailhead.

49 Ferry Bluff SNA–Cactus Bluff Trail

This short hike follows a steep grade to the top of Cactus Bluff for outrageous views of the Wisconsin River (and the site of an infamous beach).

Lake or river: Wisconsin River
Photogenic factor: 5
Distance: 0.8 mile out and back (including spur trail to the river)
Difficulty: Easy to base of the bluff, then a short, steep grade to the top
Hiking time: About 1 hour
Trail surface: Hard-packed dirt path

Other trail users: None
Canine compatibility: Leashed pets allowed
Land status: State land
Fees and permits: None
Maps: DNR maps; USGS Mazomanie
Trail contacts: Wisconsin Department of Natural Resources, 101 S. Webster St., Madison 53707; (888) 936-7463; dnr.wi.gov

Finding the trailhead: From the junction of US 12 and WI 60 west of Sauk City, follow WI 60 southwest 4.3 miles to Ferry Bluff Road and turn left. Follow Ferry Bluff Road 1.5 miles to the parking area and trailhead. **Trailhead GPS:** N43 23.976' / W89 81.012'

The Hike

Looming more than 300 feet above the meeting of Honey Creek and the Wisconsin River, Ferry and Cactus Bluffs make up a bulbous sandstone escarpment capped with dolomite and hardy cliff vegetation. Remnants of ancient prairies are visible, and the bluff's steep slopes are draped with majestic white and red oaks, blended with hackberry, basswood, hickory, elm, and stalwart ironwood. A diversity of ferns, including the bulblet fern, and other groundcover flora layer the forest floor.

As expected in this region of valleys, bluffs, and floodplains, raptors are common sights. This was once the site of an active peregrine falcon aerie and remains a very busy place for roosting bald eagles in winter. Keep your eyes on the skies and you're likely to spot these regal birds. Note that the area is closed from mid-November to April 1 to protect the roosting balds.

In Civil War times the base of the bluff was the site of a ferryboat landing, where an enterprising pair transported people and all manner of goods across the river with a rowboat. In more recent times the other side of the river saw a different kind of activity. For decades, Mazo Beach was *the* place to go for nudists and an all-around party crowd, with more than a few nefarious goings-on, tomfoolery, and shenanigans. Officials closed the beach in 2016 so the view today from Ferry Bluff is far more languid than in days of yore.

From the trailhead, follow the path along the river to a fork at the base of the bluff. The riverside option wanders a short distance further to a dead end. To reach the blufftop, take the right fork and hike up through the oak forest. Expect some

Wisconsin River from atop Cactus Bluff. DENICE BREAUX

Hiking the trail on a rainy day. DENICE BREAUX

MAZOMANIE BOTTOMS

Old river channels dissect an enormous area of floodplain forest along the Ferry Bluff stretch of the Wisconsin River. The woods are filled with giant cottonwoods, silver maple, basswood, ash, willow, and river birch. Sandbars and ephemeral pools host an incredible diversity of wildlife, especially the thousands of migrating birds. Visitors here can spot several species of warblers, winter wrens, brown creepers, woodpeckers, and bald eagles. Seasonal flooding consistently alters the beach areas and accompanying activity of wild critters.

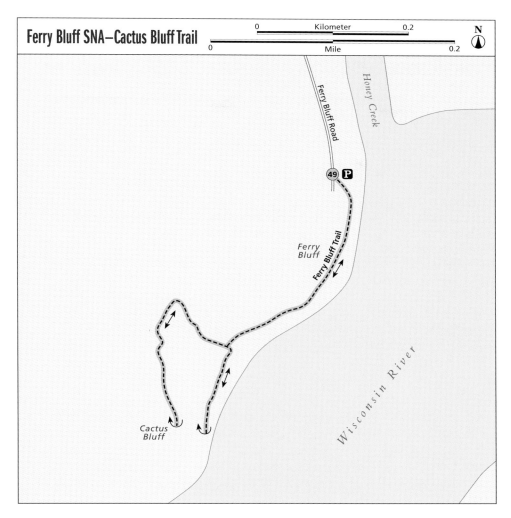

steep sections near the top, but once up there it is difficult to leave. This and adjacent bluffs are *500 million* years old, and from the top of Cactus Bluff you are treated to 8-mile views of the Wisconsin River, Wisconsin Heights Battle Ground, Sauk City and Prairie du Sac, and the Mazomanie Floodplain Forest.

Grand sights in all directions, to be sure. After lingering awhile turn back and follow the same route back to the trailhead.

Miles and Directions

0.0 From the trailhead, hike southwest 0.2 mile to the junction with a spur trail to the river. Head down there to the water's edge. (Jump in if you need a refresh.) Then hike back to the junction and follow the path uphill.

0.4 Reach the top of the bluff. Ogle the views and then retrace your tracks.

0.8 Arrive back at the trailhead.

50 Devil's Lake State Park

Wisconsin's largest state park hosts some of the Midwest's most exquisite scenery and balcony views from high bluffs. Have it all and more on the short East Bluff Trail loop. Chase it with an optional circumnavigation of the entire lake for extra exhilarating miles.

Lake or river: Devil's Lake
Photogenic factor: 5
Distance: 2.6-mile lollipop (3.1 miles if completing the spur trail to Balanced Rock)
Difficulty: Moderate
Hiking time: About 2 hours
Trail surface: Hard-packed dirt and gravel path, with a short section of aged asphalt

Other trail users: None
Canine compatibility: Leashed pets allowed
Land status: State park
Fees and permits: Vehicle pass required
Maps: State park maps; USGS Baraboo
Trail contacts: Devil's Lake State Park, 55975 Park Rd., Baraboo 53913; (608) 356-8301; dnr.wi.gov/topic/parks/name/devilslake/

Finding the trailhead: From I-90/94, follow US 12 south 10 miles to exit 219 (South Boulevard). Turn left to WI 136 and head south 3 miles to the park entrance.
Trailhead GPS: N43 42.844' / W89 72.655'

The Hike

Nearly 2 billion years in the making, the Baraboo Hills were at one time higher than the Rockies, and as is common throughout much of Wisconsin, ice played a big role in the lumpy topography we see today. The dramatic 500-foot bluffs surrounding Devil's Lake were sculpted by a monstrously thick glacier, and the lake itself formed by terminal moraines that plugged gaps in the bluffs at the north and south ends. Incredible. I'm forever fascinated by the unfathomable power of glaciers and find myself thinking about ice every time I hike in this area.

The stop-in-your-tracks beauty of this place appeals to lots of other people as well. From the start of the twentieth century, in fact, the area has attracted hordes of visitors, and today, more than 1 million visitors a year pour into the park. The good news is it's relatively easy to steer clear of the throngs via trails less traveled. Even better news is the park is also packed with around 100 bird species, nearly 900 plant species, and a who's who of Wisconsin mammals like white-tailed deer, gray wolves, flying squirrels, red foxes, raptors of various ilk, coyotes, rabbits, and beavers.

From the trailhead, follow the wide dirt path/road to the junction with the East Bluff Woods Trail. Veer left and start climbing through a wildly scenic maple-mixed hardwood forest. There's a full mile and 500 feet of elevation gain ahead of you so just settle into a comfortable rhythm and enjoy this beautiful place.

Devil's Lake State Park

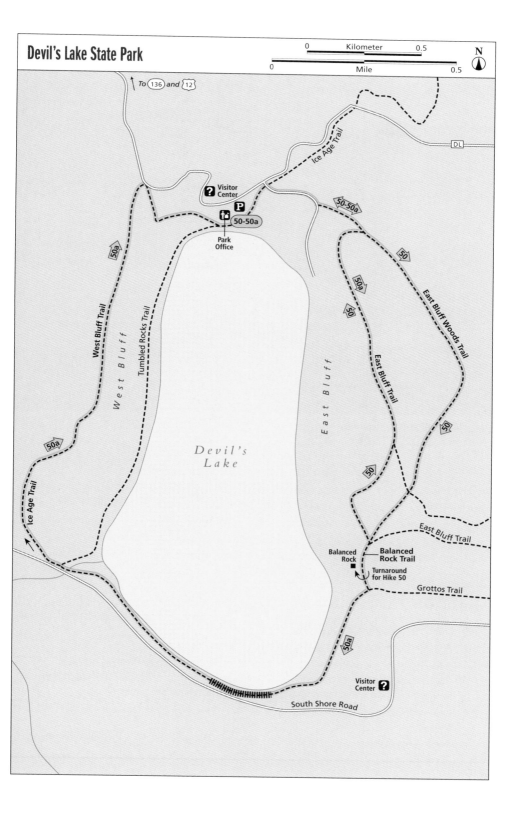

0 — Kilometer — 0.5
0 — Mile — 0.5

N

To ⬡136 and ⬡12

Ice Age Trail

DL

? Visitor Center

🅿

50-50a

Park Office

50-50a

West Bluff Trail

West Bluff

Tumbled Rocks Trail

50a

50a

Devil's Lake

East Bluff Woods Trail

50

50a

50

East Bluff

East Bluff Trail

50

50

Ice Age Trail

50a

East Bluff Trail

Balanced Rock

Balanced Rock Trail

Turnaround for Hike 50

Grottos Trail

50a

Visitor Center ?

South Shore Road

Great views of Devil's Lake from the top of the east ridge. DENICE BREAUX

After trekking across the top of the bluff, you'll reach a junction with the Balanced Rock Trail. It's only about 0.2 mile (but fairly steep) to this remarkable geologic oddity and worth the trip if you're up for it. Back at the junction, follow the East Bluff Trail northbound. Linger at the overlooks for outrageous views of mile-long Devil's Lake far below. ***Note:*** Be careful! A moment of inattention or a misstep can lead to a long fall and bad things will happen. Enjoy the views safely.

From here, the trail begins a long descent with a few relatively steep sections on its way to the valley floor and the junction left back to the trailhead.

Miles and Directions

- **0.0** From the trailhead, hike southeast on the dirt road.
- **0.1** At the junction with the East Bluff Woods Trail, veer left.
- **1.4** At the junction with Balanced Rock Trail, turn left and descend to see the rock. The main route turns right, climbing for a short distance to several overlooks with life-list views of the lake way down there and the west and south bluffs. Head back on East Bluff Trail.
- **2.5** Arrive at the hike's first junction with the East Bluff Woods Trail. Turn left to return to the trailhead.
- **2.6** Arrive at the trailhead.

50a Devil's Lake Roundabout

See map on page 207.
Distance: 5.1-mile loop

Difficulty: Difficult
Hiking time: About 3 hours

Finding the trailhead: From I-90/94, follow US 12 south 10 miles to exit 219 (South Boulevard). Turn left to WI 136 and head south 3 miles to the park entrance.
Trailhead GPS: N43 42.844' / W89 72.655'

The Hike

For the adventurous spirit, it's tough to resist making a day of it on a circumnavigation of the lake, taking in lofty views from the soaring east and west bluffs. From the same trailhead as the East Bluff hike above, follow the East Bluff Trail southbound to Balanced Rock and then veer right to loop past the tangle of concession stands and lots of people.

A short section of boardwalk on the lake's far southern tip angles up toward the boat ramp and the junction with the Tumbled Rocks and West Bluff Trails. Follow the West Bluff Trail up a long grade to the top and plan on stopping many times to ogle outrageously beautiful views of the lake and rolling hills to the east. The trail squiggles up for a while before eventually descending to North Shore Road. A right turn here leads past the northern beach and concessions, with a final curve back north and east to the trailhead.

Miles and Directions

0.0 From the trailhead, hike southeast on the dirt road.

0.1 At the junction with the East Bluff Trail, turn right.

1.2 At the junction with the Balanced Rock Trail, turn right and descend to see the rock.

1.6 At the junction with the Grottos Trail, turn right and hike past the south-shore area.

3.0 Merge with the West Bluff Trail and start a long, steady climb to the top of the bluff. (This is also part of the Ice Age Trail.)

4.4 At the junction with North Shore Road, turn right and follow the trail past the beach to the upper parking areas and the east trailhead.

5.1 Arrive at the trailhead.

51 Gibraltar Rock State Natural Area— Ice Age Trail

This hike to the top of Gibraltar Rock rewards with exhilarating, panoramic views of the Wisconsin River Valley, Lake Wisconsin, and the far-off Baraboo Hills.

Lake or river: Wisconsin River
Photogenic factor: 4+
Distance: 1.4-mile lollipop loop
Difficulty: Easy to moderate
Hiking time: About 1 hour
Trail surface: Hard-packed dirt path with scattered rocks
Other trail users: None

Canine compatibility: Leashed pets allowed
Land status: State land
Fees and permits: None
Maps: State park maps; USGS Madison
Trail contacts: Wisconsin DNR, 101 S. Webster St., Madison 53707; (888) 936-7463; dnr.wi .gov/topic/lands/naturalareas/

Finding the trailhead: From Lodi, head north on WI 113 4 miles to CR V. Turn left and go west 1.1 miles to Gibraltar Rock Road and follow this road south 0.2 mile to parking and the trailhead. **Trailhead GPS:** N43. 34.948' / W89 59.933'

The Hike

Five miles northwest of Lodi, Gibraltar Rock is our humble midwestern counterpart to the fabled Rock of Gibraltar on the southern tip of Europe's Iberian Peninsula. To ancient peoples, the Rock was known as the limits of the known world, and early sailors were warned not to travel beyond. The looming promontory is also featured in Greek mythology as one of the Pillars of Hercules. Coming upon the great mountain Atlas while carrying out his penance, Hercules didn't feel like climbing over it and instead broke it apart with his bare hands, forming today's Strait of Gibraltar, which links the Mediterranean Sea and the Atlantic.

Nothing quite that dramatic in Wisconsin's 1800s, but the intrepid Richmond family pushed through their own adversity and settled the land around Gibraltar Rock. The site became a State Natural Area in 1969, and thanks to the efforts of dedicated preservation groups including the Ice Age Trail Alliance, modern-day explorers can trek to the top of this 1,200-foot forested butte and score some of the most ravishing views in the state.

From the trailhead, follow the Ice Age Trail and yellow blazes into a dense mixed-hardwood forest of maple, oak, hickory, ash, and other mixed hardwoods. (Some hikers choose the old DNR access road, but it's much steeper and the aged asphalt is a crumbling, unfriendly route.) Climbing steadily upward, the trail follows stone steps through scattered boulder piles that look like scenes from *The Lord of the Rings*.

Grand views from Gibraltar's summit. Denice Breaux

Rust-colored needles from slender pines cover the rocks and trail, softening footsteps and lending a soft glow to the place.

Closer to the top of this 200-foot sandstone butte, the trail switchbacks into a grove of aged red cedars, the air heavy with their rich fragrance. Just past the trees' gnarled branches, the world below opens its arms wide. Indeed, some of the most breathlessly beautiful views in all of Wisconsin are seen right here from the top of this rock. The valley unfurls in an elegant patchwork of farmsteads and fields and the

THE MERRIMAC FERRY

In Wisconsin one way to describe summer is the time between "ice-out" and "ice-in," which for non-natives generally means anything that happens that's not winter. Ah, it's usually not that bad but it *is* the only time you can ride the Merrimac Ferry across the Wisconsin River between Merrimac and Okee. The *Colsac III* is the latest iteration of the first ferry boats to cross as far back as the early 1800s. Today's free ferry winches itself across the river via submerged cables on a 7-minute trip from one side to the other and is both a tourist attraction and vital link in the state's highway system.

blue line of the Wisconsin River. Turkey vultures, bald eagles, and hawks cruise the thermals near the cliff, no doubt enjoying the views as much as we do. The Merrimac Ferry is also visible in the distance and it's a pretty cool addition to this real-life mural. Gibraltar is a popular place in summer, but start early to score plenty of peace and quiet.

Frame-worthy views of the Wisconsin River valley. Denice Breaux

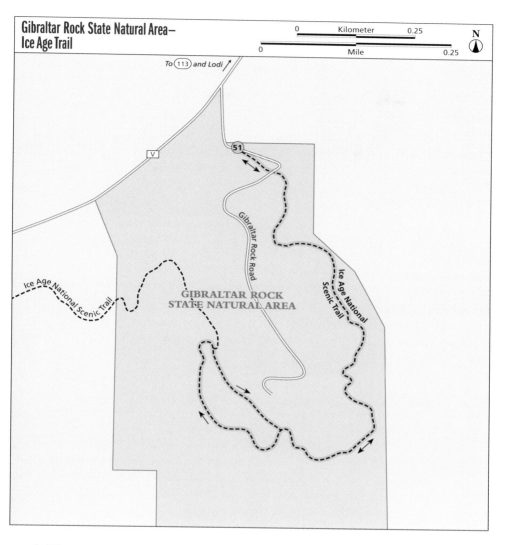

To ⑴⑶ and Lodi

V

51

Gibraltar Rock Road

Ice Age National Scenic Trail

GIBRALTAR ROCK
STATE NATURAL AREA

Ice Age National Scenic Trail

0 — Kilometer — 0.25
0 — Mile — 0.25

N

Miles and Directions

0.0 From the trailhead, hike into the beauteous forest on a gentle grade past the junction with the old access road. Keep on heading uphill. Near the top, the trail does a couple of lazy switchbacks.

0.75 Turn left here to start the blufftop loop, passing through cedars to wondrous views of the Wisconsin River Valley. Be careful near the edge and stay with the IAT as it traces the edge at 1,234 feet.

1.0 At the junction with the white-blazed spur trail, turn right.

1.1 At the junction with the IAT again, at the top of the switchbacks, turn left for the return to the trailhead.

1.4 Arrive at the trailhead.

52 Black River State Forest

Looking for way-out-there solitude? Black River State Forest is filled with it, like this relaxing loop hike at Big Bear Flowage in the company of sandhill cranes and bald eagles.

Lake or river: Big Bear and Wilson Marsh Flowages
Photogenic factor: 4
Distance: 1.3-mile loop
Difficulty: Easy
Hiking time: About 1 hour
Trail surface: Dirt and grass doubletrack
Other trail users: None
Canine compatibility: Leashed pets allowed

Land status: State forest
Fees and permits: None
Maps: State forest maps; USGS Black River Falls
Trail contacts: Black River State Forest, W10325 Highway 12, Black River 54615; (715) 284-1400; dnr.wi.gov/topic/StateForests/blackRiver/

Finding the trailhead: Exit I-94 at Black River Falls and follow WI 54 8 miles east to Wildcat Road. Head south 0.8 mile to Battle Point Road (the first gravel forest road). Turn left, heading east 2.8 miles, and turn right at this road. Follow it 0.7 mile to the trailhead.
Trailhead GPS: N44 31.098' / W90 63.098'

The Hike

The elk are back. After a 125-year absence, elk were released in the Black River State Forest and today roam free. Twenty-two years of reintroduction efforts succeeded, and the elk population continues to increase, numbering about fifty-five in spring of 2018. The long-term goal is a 400-strong herd and officials are confident the regal animals will get there. That's good stuff, and even if you never see one, it feels great walking around these trails just knowing they're out there.

A wild and remote setting at the flowage. KENT MERHAR

Big Bear Flowage. KENT MERHAR

Herons in flight. KENT MERHAR

Others of the animal kingdom living in and roaming about this 8,000-acre forest are black bears, deer, ruffed grouse, wolves, and wild turkeys to name just a few. Red-tailed hawks, bald eagles, and a bazillion songbirds are common sights as well. Critters love it here for the unique blend of habitats found in the forest's landscape along the border of Wisconsin's ancient glaciated plains; I love it for its typically dead-calm quiet with nary another soul to be found.

This short, easy hike offers a tiny sample of what's out here in this great big world. From the trailhead, follow the dirt-and-grass doubletrack on a northwesterly heading, passing through a copse of pine/hardwood and into a stretch of tallgrasses close to the placid waters of Big Bear Flowage. The trail curves between two "lakes" of the flow-age, frequented by sandhill cranes, a variety of ducks, and other water-loving birds.

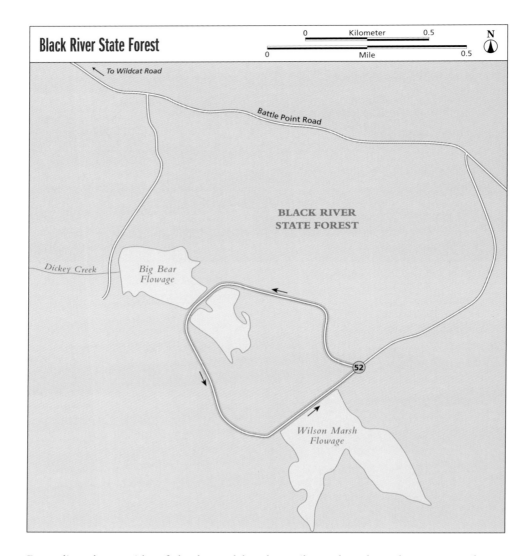

To Wildcat Road

Battle Point Road

BLACK RIVER
STATE FOREST

Dickey Creek

Big Bear
Flowage

52

Wilson Marsh
Flowage

Rounding the topside of the lower lake, the trail wanders through more woods and meets back up with the main road. Hang a left here, hike past the Wilson Marsh Flowage on your right, and in short order you'll be back at the trailhead.

Looking for more miles? Find 24 of them at the Smrekar and Wildcat trail systems just a short drive south on North Settlement Road.

Miles and Directions

0.0   From the trailhead, hike northwest on flat doubletrack.

0.5   Pass through the "highland" between the upper and lower sections of Big Bear Flowage.

1.0   Link back to the road/path back to the trailhead.

1.3   Arrive at the trailhead.

53 Lakeshore Nature Preserve—UW Madison

Muir and Leopold were here. Put your boots on the same ground as these seminal environmentalists with a relaxing hike on Lake Mendota's postcard peninsula.

Lake or river: Lake Mendota
Photogenic factor: 5
Distance: 2.0 miles for Picnic Point loop (add 0.7 mile to Frautschi Point)
Difficulty: Easy to moderate
Hiking time: 1+ hour
Trail surface: Hard-packed dirt path and some paved

Other trail users: Runners
Canine compatibility: Leashed pets allowed
Land status: University of Wisconsin
Fees and permits: None
Maps: Preserve maps; USGS Madison West
Trail contacts: Lakeshore Nature Preserve, 30 N. Mills St., Madison 53715; (608) 265-9275; lakeshorepreserve.wisc.edu

Finding the trailhead: From the north end of Camp Randall Stadium on the UW campus, follow University Avenue westbound 0.6 mile to Walnut Street. Turn right and follow Walnut north 0.5 mile to its junction with Willow Drive and continue north to University Bay Drive. Turn right and head north 0.25 mile to the preserve entrance and trailhead. **Trailhead GPS:** N43 08.427' / W89 42.868'

The Hike

Maybe it's just me, but there's something special about walking the same ground as Muir and Leopold. Both of these legendary environmental thinkers studied at UW and their influence is alive in these woods.

Lakeshore Preserve is 300 acres and more than 4 miles of splendidly scenic Lake Mendota shoreline, protecting a piece of UW-Madison's irreplaceable natural treasures. Picnic Point, the highlight of this particular hike, is a peninsula poking out nearly a full mile into Lake Mendota and arguably the most popular outdoor destination for students and Madison residents as a whole.

Today's visitors of course are far from the first to appreciate the area. Evidence of ancient peoples from 12,000 years ago has been found on the point, and the early nineteenth century saw several farmsteads sprout among the woods and open fields.

From the trailhead near University Bay Marsh, hike through a short, narrow sliver of open area and then into a forest of mixed hardwoods including maple, red oak, elm, and basswood. Along the southern edge of Picnic Point, pass a couple of fire rings (favorite locales for evening social hours) and eventually to the tip of Picnic Point. Breathtaking 180-degree views of Lake Mendota, UW's main campus, and the state capitol complex unfold from here. Loop around the point and back along the northern edge of the skinny point past Picnic Point Marsh to a junction on its western end. If you're in the mood for a short hike, turn left here and head back to the trailhead.

Idyllic hiking in the preserve. DENICE BREAUX

For the longer loop, continue northwest along the shore, with intermittent views of the lake through the dense woods. With the exception of a few gradual elevation changes; this stretch is fairly level and easygoing. You'll pass through Caretaker's Woods, an 8-acre patch of forest immediately east of Biocore Prairie. This land was once part of the sprawling estate of Edward Young, and his caretaker lived in a little house at the edge of the property. The caretaker kept busy pruning the orchard, clearing snow, and keeping an eye on sneaky university students.

The woods is named for the old caretaker's house that stood ground here a very long time ago, and the home's aged foundations are still visible today. Notice as well that some of the big oaks have wide-reaching branches; evidence that in their younger years they grew in a more open environment, which indeed this area was before the forest proper took over. Don't miss the opportunity to stroll up to the top of the hill for beauteous views of Lake Mendota.

From here, follow the path through Second Point Woods and on to Frautschi Point, the large nose of land poking out in the lake. The generous gift of this parcel to the university in late 1980s linked the university's portion of the shoreline and made the creation of the Lakeshore Nature Preserve possible.

Enjoy the point for a while and then squiggle down the path through the east side of the prairie to return to the trailhead.

Lakeshore Nature Preserve—UW Madison

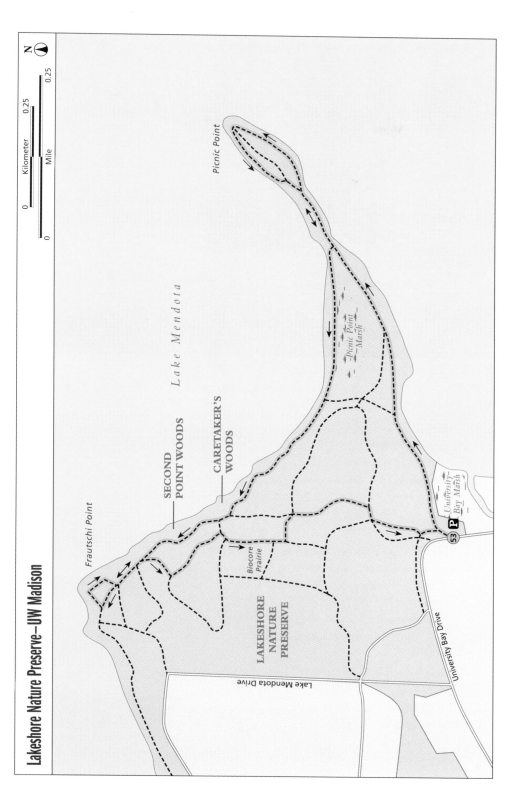

N

Kilometer
0   0.25

Mile
0   0.25

Frautschi Point

SECOND
POINT WOODS

CARETAKER'S
WOODS

Lake Mendota

Picnic Point

Picnic Point
Marsh

Biocore
Prairie

LAKESHORE
NATURE
PRESERVE

Lake Mendota Drive

University
Bay Marsh

53 P

University Bay Drive

Relaxing close-up with Lake Mendota. DENICE BREAUX

Miles and Directions

0.0 From the trailhead, hike northeast along the point for about 0.6 mile to a split in the trail and turn right. Make a counterclockwise loop around the skinny point.

1.0 Veer right at this junction.

1.6 At this junction, turn left for the short loop.

1.8 Turn right to curve back south to the trailhead.

2.0 Arrive back at the trailhead.

Option: Frautschi Point Loop directions from mile 1.6 above.

1.6 Turn right here and follow the trail along the lakeshore.

1.8 Turn right here on the short horseshoe trail at the tip of the point and right again on the other side.

1.9 Turn left here and right at the next fork just ahead.

2.0 Left turn at this junction and right at the next.

2.1 Turn left.

2.3 Turn right, heading south, passing all side trails to 2.5 miles.

2.5 Turn right.

2.6 Turn left back to the trailhead.

2.7 Arrive back at the trailhead.

54 University of Wisconsin Arboretum

This is a 1,200-acre sanctuary with decades of conservation efforts and inspiration from none other than Aldo Leopold. It's all here at the University of Wisconsin's Arboretum, tailor made for wandering, connecting, and simply being.

Lake or river: Lake Wingra
Photogenic factor: 4+
Distance: 1.8-mile loop
Difficulty: Easy
Hiking time: About 1 hour
Trail surface: Packed dirt and grass
Other trail users: None
Canine compatibility: Pets not allowed

Land status: University of Wisconsin
Fees and permits: None
Maps: UW Arboretum maps; USGS Madison West
Trail contacts: UW Arboretum, 1207 Seminole Hwy., Madison 53711; (608) 263-7888; arboretum.wisc.edu

Finding the trailhead: From I-90, follow US 12 7 miles to South Park Street and curve south just over 0.5 mile to Haywood Drive. Turn right and go 3 blocks to North Wingra Drive and head straight across to Arboretum Drive. Follow the road 1.8 miles to the parking area on the right.
Trailhead GPS: N43 04.557' / W89 42.763'

The Hike

What began as an effort to preserve open space and provide a quiet place to escape the city eventually inspired the entirely new idea of ecological restoration, driven in large part by the commitment of Aldo Leopold. One of the most influential figures in environmental ethics and the wilderness conservation movement, Leopold's ideals are alive on the pages of *A Sand County Almanac*, widely regarded as the most important book on the environment ever published. He was also a founding member of the Wilderness Society, a professor of game management at UW, and a proponent of a vibrant arboretum with focus on reestablishing original Wisconsin landscapes like oak savannas and tallgrass prairies.

To that end, for six years beginning in 1935, crews from the Civilian Conservation Corps worked tirelessly to begin restoring the area's natural ecosystems, and the Arb today includes more than 1,200 acres in Madison, as well as outstate locations, all working to preserve land and restore ecological communities.

With such esteemed lineage and decades of successful environmental efforts, it's hard not to be filled with pride and gratitude walking these trails. From the Wingra Springs parking area, follow the path north past ancient effigy mounds and take the path north and west to the N5 trail marker for a great, up-close view of Big Spring and its perpetual flow into the lake. Hike east from here to K4, turn south through splendiferous Wingra Woods, and cross the road at K1. A gentle curve leads to G5

Trail running at the Arb. DENICE BREAUX

and a left turn into the enchanting Lost City Forest. The trail wanders through here to L4 and a right turn bends around to L3. Go right again, pass F2, and hike along Juniper Knoll (don't miss a quick side trip on the short path to Teal Pond on the right) to F6. From here the trail heads due north between Gallistel Woods and the visitor center garden areas. At G7, take the short spur trail left and cross the road back to the trailhead.

I have a hunch you'd like to see more of this wonderful place and you're in luck because the Arb has 15 more miles of trails to explore, and no trip here is complete without touring the visitor center or tagging along on a guided tour of the gardens. Check the sidebar for more scoop.

THE GARDENS

The UW Arboretum delights the senses with three outrageously beautiful and ecologically diverse garden areas, including an inspiring example of a wildly successful native plant community restoration. Highlighting the field is the 35-acre Longenecker Horticultural Garden, internationally known for its 2,500 different plant species and North America's largest display of lilacs. The Viburnum Garden hosts 3 acres of nearly 100 species of its namesake plant and 110 of arborvitae. The Wisconsin Native Plant Garden includes fifteen separate gardens with hundreds of native plant species and fascinating displays of ecological restoration.

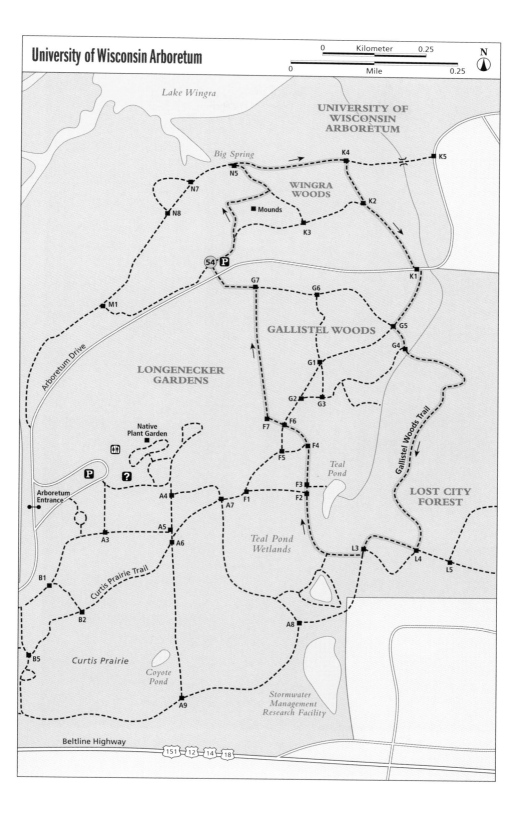

University of Wisconsin Arboretum

0   Kilometer   0.25

0   Mile   0.25

N

Lake Wingra

UNIVERSITY OF
WISCONSIN
ARBORETUM

Big Spring

N5   K4   K5

N7   WINGRA
WOODS   K2

N8   Mounds   K3

54 P   K1

G7   G6   G5

M1   GALLISTEL WOODS   G4

LONGENECKER
GARDENS   G1   G2   G3

Arboretum Drive

Native
Plant Garden   F7   F6   G3

F5   F4

P   Teal
Pond

Arboretum
Entrance   A4   A7   F1   F3   LOST CITY
FOREST

F2

A5   Gallistel Woods Trail

A3   A6   Teal Pond
Wetlands   L3   L4   L5

B1

Curtis Prairie Trail

B2   A8

B5   Curtis Prairie

Coyote
Pond

A9   Stormwater
Management
Research Facility

Beltline Highway

151 12 14 18

Fall-color hiking. DENICE BREAUX

Peaceful lakeside setting. DENICE BREAUX

Miles and Directions

0.0 From the trailhead, hike north in and around the effigy mounds and then follow the path northwest to trail marker N5 for a look at Big Spring. Continue the route east from here.

0.3 At the junction with trail marker K4, turn right to pass through Wingra Woods.

0.6 Road crossing at Arboretum Drive.

0.7 At the junction with trail marker G5, turn left to drop down through Lost City Forest.

1.1 At the junction with marker L4, turn right.

1.2 Turn right at marker L3. Continue straight then curve to the left to marker F7.

1.5 At the junction with marker F7, turn right and skirt the arboretum's gardens on your left.

1.7 At the junction with marker G7, turn left to cross the road and head toward the trailhead.

1.8 Arrive at the trailhead.

55 Pheasant Branch Conservancy

A quiet creek, dense forest, and a wandering path combine to make Pheasant Branch a perfect in-city escape with different trail options to match your vibe for the day.

Lake or river: Pheasant Branch Creek
Photogenic factor: 4
Distance: 2.8 miles out and back
Difficulty: Easy
Hiking time: About 1 hour
Trail surface: Packed gravel and paved
Other trail users: Cyclists, runners
Canine compatibility: Leashed pets allowed with permit

Land status: County park
Fees and permits: None
Maps: County and conservancy maps; USGS Madison West
Trail contacts: Friends of Pheasant Branch Conservancy, PO Box 628242, Middleton 53562; (608) 224-3730; pheasantbranch.org

Finding the trailhead: From US 12, exit at Airport Road/CR M and head east 1.1 miles to Frank Lloyd Wright Avenue. Turn left and then right on Pheasant Branch Road. Follow this road 0.7 mile to the parking area and trailhead. **Trailhead GPS:** N43 11.424' / W89 49.101'

The Hike

It might look unassuming on the surface, but the Pheasant Branch watershed drains 24 square miles of land in and around the Middleton area. Many springs in this region are recharged by water carried through many layers of sediment and bedrock and all told, the springs, marsh, and lake are one extensive ecosystem.

Did you know that the Pheasant Branch springs provide 2.6 million gallons of water to the marsh and adjacent Lake Mendota every single day? Impressive, but the bad news is lots more very large springs were lost to (shocker) development in the Madison area. The springs' recharge zones were paved with roads or covered with buildings or parking lots and poked with hundreds of wells to capture groundwater for a swelling population. Fortunately, planners are doing their best to preserve what the Pheasant Branch area has left because after all, we'd be lost without it.

What is the Pheasant Branch Conservancy all about? The short version is it is a highly significant natural area hosting a critical wetland marsh, open water areas, natural springs, prairies, meadows, wooded hills, and forest. That's a lot of great stuff and locals can be grateful this place is here and so close at hand to enjoy. Thousands of volunteers pitch in to help make the conservancy tick, cutting invasive species, planting prairie seeds, implementing prescribed burns, and diving in to various construction projects.

I can't say enough good things about this wonderful place. The Hill alone is steeped in history. The one significant rise in elevation is made of a prairie environment that

Trail through the trees. DENICE BREAUX

The trail passes through serene settings like this. DENICE BREAUX

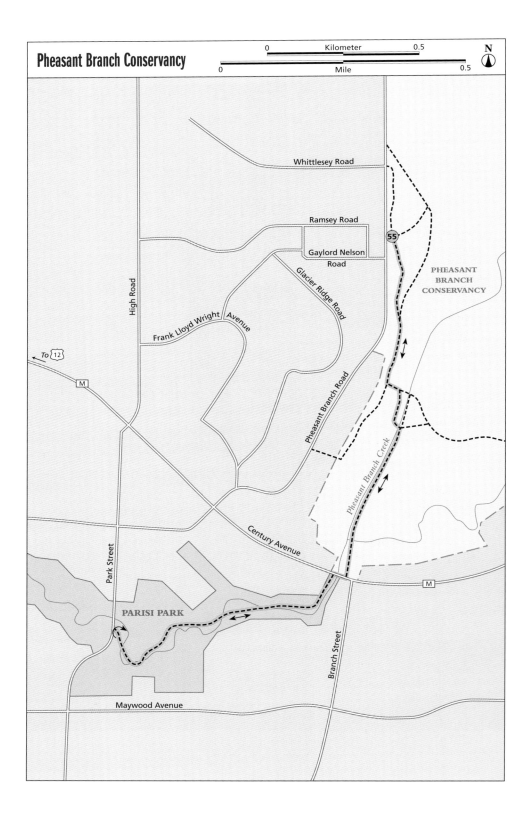

Pheasant Branch Conservancy

0   Kilometer   0.5

0   Mile   0.5

N

Whittlesey Road

Ramsey Road

Gaylord Nelson Road

55

PHEASANT BRANCH CONSERVANCY

High Road

Glacier Ridge Road

Frank Lloyd Wright Avenue

To 12

M

Pheasant Branch Road

Pheasant Branch Creek

Century Avenue

Park Street

M

PARISI PARK

Branch Street

Maywood Avenue

Pheasant Branch Creek. DENICE BREAUX

dates back several thousand years! I highly recommend heading to pheasantbranch
.org to immerse yourself in the group's detailed and info-packed website to learn
about this local gem. Then get out there and be in it!

From the trailhead on Pheasant Branch Road, hike south on the wide gravel trail
to its junction with the creek and follow the creek south to Century Avenue. The
trail changes personality from a wide thoroughfare to narrow and intimate and it's
just plain fun to be out here. It's hard not to feel like you're way out in a wilderness
somewhere.

Across the road, the trail squiggles through a scenically vibrant corridor, crossing
the creek several times on the way to the Parisi Park area. The path keeps going and I
urge you to keep exploring but today, this hike turns back here and retraces the trail
to its start.

Miles and Directions

0.0 Hike south from the trailhead through dense forest.

0.3 Turn left at this junction and make a quick right to reach the first creek crossing.

0.4 Turn right here and parallel the creek all the way to Century Avenue.

0.7 At the junction with Century Avenue, go right to meet the continuation of the trail across
the road.

1.4 Arrive at the turnaround point in the Parisi Park area.

2.8 Arrive back at the trailhead.

56 Governor Dodge State Park

This hike is like traveling through time, in the same area where Wisconsin's first governor helped keep the peace between Native Americans and early European settlers.

Lake or river: Twin Valley and Cox Hollow Lakes
Photogenic factor: 4+
Distance: 3.5-mile loop
Difficulty: Moderate with a few steep grades
Hiking time: About 90 minutes
Trail surface: Hard-packed dirt and paved
Other trail users: None
Canine compatibility: Leashed pets allowed

Land status: State park
Fees and permits: Vehicle pass required
Maps: State park maps; USGS Pleasant Ridge
Trail contacts: Governor Dodge State Park, 4175 Highway 23 N., Dodgeville 53533; (608) 935-2315; dnr.wi.gov/topic/parks/name/govdodge

Finding the trailhead: From Dodgeville, travel north on WI 23 3.2 miles to the park entrance. Take the first right past the entrance station and follow it 2.6 miles to the parking area and trailhead at the Cox Hollow beach/picnic area. **Trailhead GPS:** N43 01.501' / W90 10.508'

The Hike

Way, way back in the day, 8,000 years ago, the earliest peoples in this area made winter camps beneath the protection of overhangs of high sandstone cliffs. When the bitter cold receded, they moved to more open prairie areas to hunt bison and related critters for sustenance.

These hardy people did not know of, and had no use for, the great seams of lead ore buried in the ground beneath them. Indeed, this underground booty was spread throughout the area south of today's Wisconsin River, and in the 1820s European miners discovered it and began arriving here in droves. One of the first big finds was in Cox Hollow, a short distance south of the present-day park boundary.

To no one's real surprise, hordes of miners descended upon the area, and inevitable conflicts broke out between them and the Ho Chunk Indians, who had worked the mines long before. In a stroke of good fortune, General Henry Dodge was one of the area's original white settlers, and he was a lightning rod for establishing peace among everyone in the area. Dodge would go on to become Wisconsin's first territorial governor.

Much later the 160-acre Henry Larson farmstead was presented to the state and soon turned into the first lands of what eventually became Governor Dodge State Park. A decade later officials built an earthen dam across Mill Creek that created Cox Hollow Lake, and the park soon evolved into one of the state's most popular recreation destinations.

A weir regulates flow on Twin Valley Lake. DENICE BREAUX

Twin Valley Lake through the trees. DENICE BREAUX

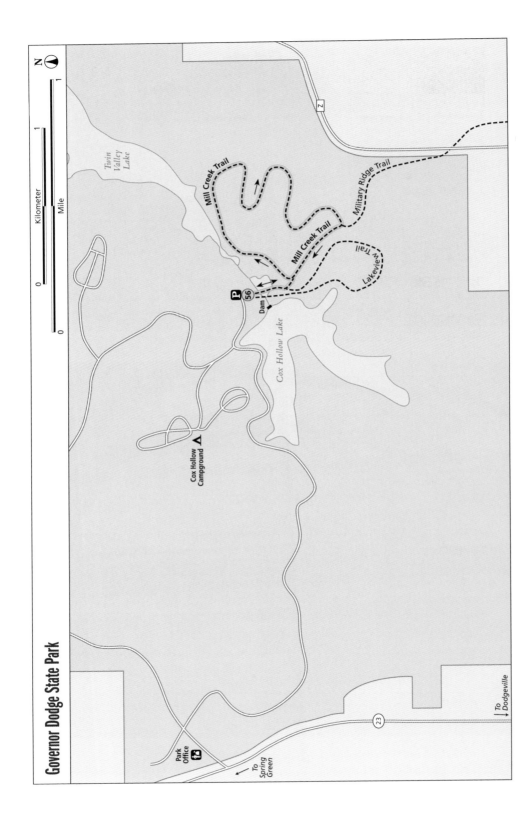

Governor Dodge State Park

Gone fishin' at the park. DENICE BREAUX

Traveling to the park today, visitors will notice miles of open plains and agriculture land until coming upon the park, which is in effect an island of verdant hills and valleys and bluffs dating back 450 million years. Enormous inland seas covered this area and deposited untold layers of sand before retreating. After that, wind and flowing water carved deep valleys into the hardened sandstone to make what we see here today.

Start hiking south from the trailhead across the confluence of Cox Hollow and Twin Valley Lakes. Much of this trail is mowed grass, with sections of singletrack as it winds through meadows and wooded valleys. You'll get stellar views of the lakes on the mostly level trail, but expect a few steep grades to make it interesting. As a bonus, the path also provides easy access to Military Ridge Trail when you're up for an unforgettable bike ride.

A left turn at the first junction takes you along the shore of Twin Valley Lake and then to a long, loping S turn in the woods. At the junction with the Military Ridge Trail, turn right to head back to the trailhead. The trailhead area is full of alternate activities like fishing, swimming, and kayaking or canoeing. There is also convenient access to the Lakeview, Pine Cliff, and the much longer Meadow Valley Trails.

Miles and Directions

0.0 Hike past the confluence of the two lakes and turn left at the first junction.

2.3 At the junction with the Military Ridge Trail, turn right.

3.5 Arrive back at the trailhead.

Hike Index

Meet the Author

Northland-bred scribe and self-propelled recreation junkie **Steve Johnson** grew up roaming the northern lakes and forest regions of Minnesota and Wisconsin and brings four generations of proud family heritage to this exciting book. An avid hiker and cyclist, Steve can usually be found on a hiking trail in the woods somewhere, or with his bike on a wide open road. With a spare hour or five, he is outdoors and in tune with nature's finest.

Author of nearly twenty books and regular contributor to *Backpacker* and other regional magazines across the country, some of Steve's other work includes two editions of *Best Bike Rides Minneapolis–St. Paul, Loop Hikes Colorado, Bicycling Wisconsin, Mountain Biking Minnesota*, and spin-off sporting events projects. Don't miss his new children's book, *Jack & Lauren in The Big Bog*. Steve lives and writes in far north Wisconsin and southeastern Minnesota.

Meet the Photographers

A native Californian, writer-photographer **Denice Breaux** is a recent Twin Cities transplant, and what better way to get acquainted with the Midwest than plunging into Wisconsin's glorious outdoors? Along the way she has become intimately familiar with chilblains, chiggers, and voracious mosquitoes, a few things not experienced on the West Coast. See more images from this book at Denice's website, denice breauxphoto.com. Her portfolio of stock images can be viewed at istockphoto.com/portfolio/DeniceBreaux.

Kent Merhar is a semiprofessional photographer with a career in health-care administration. His focus is landscape photography. When he's not outdoors hiking or enjoying a long weekend at the cabin, he's at his Minneapolis home with his partner and dog. See more of his work at facebook.com/unknownlimitsphotography.

THE TEN ESSENTIALS OF HIKING

American Hiking Society

American Hiking Society recommends you pack the "Ten Essentials" every time you head out for a hike. Whether you plan to be gone for a couple of hours or several months, make sure to pack these items. Become familiar with these items and know how to use them. Learn more at **AmericanHiking.org/hiking-resources**

1. Appropriate Footwear

6. Safety Items (light, fire, and a whistle)

2. Navigation

7. First Aid Kit

3. Water (and a way to purify it)

8. Knife or Multi-Tool

4. Food

9. Sun Protection

5. Rain Gear & Dry-Fast Layers

10. Shelter